Honest and Real

An Essential Guidebook to Drama-Free Human Resources

Praise for Karen A. Young and for *Honest and Real*

"I love this book and it is a MUST-READ for anyone who owns a small business and doesn't have an HR department. If more people would read *Honest and Real*, fewer CEOs would lose sleep over their personnel issues."

Peter Margaritis, CSP, CPA
Author, Improv Virtuoso, Keynote Speaker, Podcaster

"One of most practical and friendly HR handbooks I've ever seen. Karen does a fantastic job of projecting a laser focus on keeping your HR function running smoothly. Time is the one item in our arsenal that we don't have more of, and this book will make any small business rapidly move forward in scaling their HR function."

Dave Gruno
CEO, Shipley Energy

"Karen has hit the bullseye with *Honest and Real*. It's the ultimate HR reference for every small business (or larger business that has a small HR department). She's right when she says, 'HR isn't rocket science,' but acknowledges what you don't know can hurt you. Don't be fooled by its easy-to-read-and-understand format. This book will be the first place I reach for HR advice going forward."

Ira S. Wolfe

Chief Googlization Officer, Success Performance Solutions

"Karen Young is both an award-winning human resources leader and a dedicated, approachable expert on the full range of human resources priorities. She understands and engages fully on both the compliance side of HR and the culture side of it as well, which is why clients gain such incredible benefit from the services delivered by Karen and her team at HR Resolutions."

W. Douglas Wendt

Senior Partner, Wendt Partners

"A well-written and organized book that should be on every HR manager's desk! It should definitely be considered as required reading for college-level HR classes as well."

Nikki Wenrich

HR Analyst, Commonwealth of Pennsylvania, HR Service Center

"Karen Young's book shares her common sense and practical guidance. Our firm appreciated the thought and expertise she provided as our HR consultant, and it's wonderful to have Karen's advice in the form of a book to share with our employees and clients."

Debby Abel

President, Abel Personnel

"We have worked with Karen and HR Resolutions to implement the systems outlined in this book, and have found we have a more streamlined onboarding process with our new hires, as well as an excellent, neutral resource for our staff members who may have questions or concerns. We consider Karen a part of our senior management team when it comes to her expertise in all things HR."

Tony Darcangelo
CFO, Credo Technology Solutions

"Our firm works with Karen Young on our human resources matters, and her guidance gives us peace of mind that we are on track to do what is best for our employees and keep us in compliance with the regulators. Karen's book does a great job of putting you on the path for that same peace of mind."

Tom Moul
CFO and Principal, Stambaugh Ness, PC

"I've been blessed to know Karen professionally and personally for more than a decade. Her passion for all things HR is undeniable and contagious. She's always up for a great debate over best practice or strategy of an issue. She has a phenomenal depth of human resources and business knowledge. I'm honored and privileged to have her as a mentor, friend, and guide."

Melissa Washington, PHR
Senior Specialist – Core Talent Services, Deloitte

"How I wish this book existed when I became an 'accidental HR leader' years ago! I have been to several workshops and trainings, but have rarely seen the complicated HR discipline presented in such an easy-to-consume and empowering format as it is here in Karen Young's *Honest and Real*. HR is wonderful and strange. We wear so many hats, and that keeps it endlessly interesting.

However, regardless of the hat, we are also running scared most days about the obscene number of things that could go wrong. Using Karen's strategies, any fear you have about HR will turn into a quiet confidence. She provides the background and tools to help you maximize your workforce's performance and improve business results. After reading her book, anyone with the right attitude can do this. You can too!"

Stacey Oliver-Knappe
HR Speaker, Author, and Owner of The Customer Service Gurus

"This book is a must-have for anyone who owns or manages a small business or small organization. And regardless of our organization's size, we all need to understand HR issues and practices. The world of business and not-for-profit today is fast paced, with a never-ending need to stay on top of issues, new regulations, developing the best talent, and tackling challenges on the horizon. We all have our own toolboxes — those resources and people we rely on to help be successful. Add Karen's book to your operational toolbox … it's a must-have for any owner, manager, or aspiring leader! Like Karen, her book is straight-forward — one of the most practical and user-friendly HR handbooks available."

David Black
Retired President & CEO, Harrisburg Regional Chamber and CREDC

"This is one of the most practical and friendly HR handbooks for small business owners. It provides excellent go-to resources and practical advice. If more people would read Karen Young's book, fewer companies would face employment discrimination and wage collection lawsuits. I intend to recommend Karen's book to all my small-business clients."

Oleg N. Feldman, Esq.
CPA, Business Law Attorney and Founder of Lexern Law Group, Ltd.

"Even those of us with HR backgrounds can benefit in powerful and distinct ways from Karen Young's insights about what she calls 'drama-free HR.' Before starting my own business, I spent 10 years in HR and Organizational Development within the startup world — either inside the department or as a consultant. Now, having a small business of my own and being out of the corporate world for so long, I have a lot to learn from Karen, whose advice is practical and organized, and who challenges me to be the best CEO by leading with intention and authenticity. I highly recommend *Honest and Real* to anyone who owns or leads within a small- or mid-sized organization!"

Janel Dyan
Founder and CEO of Janel Dyan, Inc., Author of *Story. Style. Brand. -- Why Corporate Results Are a Matter of Personal Style*

An Essential Guidebook to Drama-Free Human Resources

Karen A. Young
SPHR, SHRM-SCP

*Honest and Real: An Essential Guidebook for
Drama-Free Human Resources*

Copyright 2022 by Karen A. Young, SPHR, SHRM-SCP

All rights reserved.

Published by Silver Tree Publishing, a division of
Silver Tree Communications, LLC (Kenosha, WI).
www.SilverTreePublishing.com

No portion of this book may be reproduced, scanned, sold
or distributed in any printed or electronic form without
the express written permission of the author.

Editing by:
Kate Colbert

Cover design and typesetting by:
George Stevens

First edition, May 2022

ISBN: 978-1-948238-38-0

Library of Congress Control Number: 2022908384

Created in the United States of America

HR Resolutions®, Accidental HR® and RealWorld HR® are
registered trademarks of HR Resolutions and Karen A. Young. The
business concepts and taglines *Drama-Free Human Resources*
and *Drama-Free HR* are trademarks of HR Resolutions and
are not to be sued without express written permission.

*The material in this publication has been prepared and published for
informational purposes only. The information provided should be taken as the
author's opinions and experiences at the time of writing. Especially in the HR
world, legal and regulatory changes may happen overnight. As anyone in the
HR community knows, you are responsible for your own actions, and the author
and publisher accept no liability for any losses or damages that might arise
from decisions made or actions taken as a result of reading these materials. By
using these materials, you are assuming full responsibility for your actions. You
should not act or rely upon information contained in these materials without
consulting legal, accounting, or other professional advice, where appropriate
or necessary. This information should not be construed as pertaining to
specific factual circumstances or as creating any type of client relationship.*

Dedication

This book is dedicated to my loving husband, best friend, and soul-mate, Barry Young. He truly is my "other half." Without him, I would not have all the blessings in my life. *Barry: I pray I give as much to you as you give me. Thank you for the life we have!*

And as I reflect upon the gravity of this moment in our history, I would like to express my personal and heart-felt compassion and condolences to the those who lost family members and loved ones during the COVID-19 pandemic; my respect for every single first responder; my admiration for every healthcare professional; and my sadness for all the businesses that have been forced to close their doors since 2020.

Table of Contents

Prologue 1

INTRODUCTION
My Journey to HR 7
A Global Disruption 13

PART ONE
The Proper Setup 21

   1. What You Don't Know Can Hurt You 23
   2. Job Descriptions 61
   3. Handbooks 71
   4. Record Keeping 81

PART TWO
Bringing People on Board 89

   5. Recruiting 91
   6. Interviewing 107
   7. Selection 119

8. Orientation and Onboarding 129

PART THREE
Running the Ship **139**

9. Employee Relations 141

10. Payroll 149

11. Legislative Changes 163

12. Benefits Management 171

13. Safety 183

14. Evaluations and Reviews 195

PART FOUR
Parting Ways **213**

15. Terminations 215

16. Resignations 233

17. After They've Gone 241

CASE STUDY
Seeing the ROI from Good HR Practices **249**

CONCLUSION
Failure to Plan Is Planning to Fail **257**
Acknowledgments **265**
Go Beyond the Book **267**

Keep in Touch 269
About the Author 271

Prologue

Human Resources – what a fascinating profession! Well, okay, for some of us. Most people who are Accidental HR™ people, those who bear HR responsibilities at their jobs, despite not having chosen human resources as a profession — often really don't like the field at all. For example, many people who oversee HR in small businesses or start-ups are from finance (because employing people is an expense). "Numbers are nice," finance people think — numbers are logical and I know what to make of them. People? Not so much! People can be messy; even when they're being logical, they bring their own sense of logic to work. And they don't just turn off the "whole human" and turn on the "work robot" when they come through the door. They have feelings, they have drama, they have emotions. They also communicate in different ways, bring different attitudes and talents to the workplace, and give off different vibes ... for better or for worse.

People can be messy; even when they're being logical, they bring their own sense of logic to work. And they don't just turn off the "whole human" and turn on the "work robot" when they come through the door. They have feelings, they have drama, they have emotions.

HR has always been a complicated endeavor. Now add a global pandemic and other crises (like nationwide supply-chain problems and economic challenges) into the mix and, well, you know what I'm talking about. We have all experienced the unimaginable since March 2020. And there's no turning back — normal has already begun to return but it's a new normal. Frankly, it always is a "new" normal. Change is inevitable. And change changes us ... those pesky humans with all the drama and emotions and needs.

That's what brings us to this book — *Honest and Real: An Essential Guidebook for Drama-Free Human Resources*. The essence of this book was originally published in 2015 (my very first book!) and a second edition was released in early 2020, with books beginning to hit bookshelves and desks in early March 2020. Yes, the March 2020. The second edition of *Stop Knocking on My Door: Drama-Free HR to Help Grow Your Business* was released about a month before the world stopped turning. I was excited; I was ready to step on stages and take "book selfies" with adoring fans; I was poised for world domination. I was an HR expert with a new book on the subject, and I was ready to share my insights. But, alas, there was no big "launch event," no book signing, no world-premiere keynote about the contents of the book.

Suddenly, to leaders of all stripes and in every type of organization, HR mattered acutely and it mattered differently. "How do we keep our people (and our customers) safe and healthy?" "How will we get our hands on supplies so people can do their jobs?" "How do we convert most or all of our processes or work activities so they can be done from home or in socially distanced ways?" "Can we afford to pay our people during a shutdown?" My book was a primer for all the key elements of a thriving HR function, but with the whole world in crisis mode, leaders were more interested in on-site virus testing than they were in the intricacies of job descriptions or workman's comp or FMLA.

An Evolved Book for a World Forever Changed

Stop Knocking on My Door was, against all odds, a success. It has made a meaningful difference in companies, careers, and lives. If you were to read it today, in a post-pandemic business climate, you'd still find it relevant and practical and easy to apply. But my readers (you!) deserve an expanded conversation. You deserve answers to your new COVID-inspired HR questions and you deserve the benefit of the new insights I can offer after having supported many HR professionals (intentional and accidental!) through an unprecedented business era.

So here we are again, with me saying "hello again" and offering to help HR people take a fresh new look at everything we do for (and about) our people.

Rather than offering you a third edition of my first book, it's time to reimagine the content altogether. The old title no longer fit — businesses have to get down to brass tacks and lead like never before. Honest conversations about real situations will set YOUR business apart through unique and even harsh realities. Hence the new title: *Honest and Real*!

Don't get me wrong — the "old" book is still good! But the new book brings you updated information on our "new" normal. You'll find an entire chapter entitled "A Global Disruption," as well as additional content in each chapter that offers fresh insights about HR basics in a post-pandemic workplace.

Why the title? *Honest and Real: An Essential Guidebook for Drama-Free Human Resources*. What does being "*Honest and Real*" have to do with human resources? Everything. I have always believed in honest conversations with staff and colleagues. In 2020-2021, businesses learned how important these conversations were;

organizations and their teams had to fight (almost literally!) for their businesses' lives! The conversations got real ... real quick:

- Are we an essential business?
- Who are my essential employees?
- How do I keep my people safe inside the organization?
- Am I responsible for my employees' behaviors outside the organization?
- Am I entitled to their health-status information?

What does being "Honest and Real" have to do with human resources? Everything.

My job, as an HR professional, is to provide honest-and-real feedback to the leaders and employees I support. Everyone needs honest feedback to make well-informed decisions and to perform at their best. Being honest means being upfront, proactive, and not hiding. Being vulnerable is part of being honest (with yourself and with others.) And while *"Honest and Real"* sound like two words for the same thing, they're actually two vital, interrelated concepts.

Being honest is a good start, but our honesty must be relevant. Telling an employee that their recurrence as the latecomer to the morning shift at your restaurant is causing hardships for everyone else is honest; doing so without consideration for the fact that their car broke down and the local transit authority workers are on strike ignores the reality of the situation.

Real feedback recognizes that our world is messy. We need to make decisions based in reality — when it's good, when it's messy, when it's unprecedented; we need to adjust and customize to each situation we encounter. Cookie-cutter HR practices just don't, well, "cut" it. *"Honest and Real"* is a mindset that allows us to find what works ... and what is in the best interest of both the organization and the employee.

"Honest and Real" is a mindset that allows us to find what works ... and what is in the best interest of both the organization and the employee.

Honest-and-real (ahem, "HR") feedback will set you apart. Applying *Honest and Real* human resources practices will lead to a better place to work, a higher return on investment, and, most importantly, a more cohesive and efficient business!

Introduction
My Journey to HR

I started out as a music major (yep, seven instruments by the time I graduated high school!). Seriously. After just one semester and with too many classical piano practice rooms and not enough money as a performer with a degree in music, I changed my academic major to business. That's what you did if you couldn't cut it as a music major at Lebanon Valley College (or you became an education major and if I was going to teach, well … why leave music?). So business it was.

While sifting through the course catalog, looking for something to fill the one slot I had for a second semester elective, I stumbled across organizational psychology — the scientific study of human behavior in the workplace. How we discover our calling and why we're called is often a mystery. Maybe the fact that I was interested in the class description at all should have been an indication, but after a few short weeks in the class, I had found my profession!

How we discover our calling and why we're called is often a mystery.

Back then, human resources (HR) was called *personnel*. Because personnel wasn't an academic major at the time, I double-majored in business and psychology, weaving together everything I learned about business with everything I found fascinating about the mind and human behavior. (Today, it's often referred to as Human Capital Management — oh how I *loathe* that term!)

As I neared graduation, I chose to survey more than 100 personnel leaders across the United States, asking what they believed was more important: continuing my education or getting practical experience. The results were overwhelming: I was told to get some real-world experience because the only way to break into personnel was to move into the department from within a company. So to get a job in my chosen field, I needed experience. To get experience, I needed a job in my chosen field. What a marvelous Catch-22, right?!

To get a job in my chosen field, I needed experience. To get experience, I needed a job in my chosen field.

A Profession I Loved, But Without a Welcome Mat

Personnel people had to understand work and business. They had to know "what it was like on the inside." After I completed an internship in a personnel department for Hershey Entertainment and Resorts Co. (yes, "the sweetest place on earth"), HERCO wanted to keep me but didn't have anything in personnel. So they offered me a job as a front desk clerk at the famous Hotel Hershey. Still unable to get involved in managing or supporting the HR functions of a business, I moved to an assistant manager position with Wendy's and accepted responsibilities for crew scheduling and performance evaluations (as well as being thrown into employee relations with teenagers and minor labor laws!). Then, three years after graduating from college, I got my big break — working as an accounting temp, processing payrolls for a restaurant holding company. I was in.

Sometime in the mid-1980s, the name of the profession changed from "personnel" to "human resources," maybe because someone finally realized that no resource is more important to a business or its leaders than the people who work for you.

Like many of you, I fell into HR accidentally, but I *love* it.

Like many of you, I fell into HR accidentally, but I *love* it. I've had to accept that not everyone loves human resources management, but I hope that my passion for the profession will help even the most reluctant Accidental HR® manager find something to love in the field. With the vast majority of small businesses in the United States being so small that they don't have formal departments or a true C-suite, much less a dedicated, full-time HR professional, it stands to reason that there might be more "accidental HR professionals" (CEOs, owners, presidents, CFOs, managing directors, general managers, controllers, office managers) than formal HR leaders among us! And if you're one of those people who finds yourself managing the people in your organization even though you don't identify yourself as an HR person, it would behoove you to learn to love (okay, at least like) HR. In my experience, when the HR pieces are falling into place, a business starts to run like a well-oiled machine.

When the HR pieces are falling into place, a business starts to run like a well-oiled machine.

You Can't Afford to Ignore the "HR Stuff"

People always ask, "How do you deal with this 'HR stuff' every day?" I understand that a life of living, breathing, and dreaming about HR isn't for everyone. But in a small business, *someone* must handle the human resources "stuff." Often, that someone has little to no interest in human resources and/or no specific training outside of a seminar or two. And yet, that person has accidentally become responsible for their company's human resource management.

HR isn't rocket science, but it can be confusing and frustrating. It can also be rewarding and fulfilling.

HR isn't rocket science, but it can be confusing and frustrating. It can also be rewarding and fulfilling, and I've helped many people turn the corner and learn to embrace what quality HR management can do for their company (and for their state of mind). It's important to remember that you're not alone and you can, indeed, accomplish your Accidental HR™ duties while watching a company grow. When it comes to managing the "people department," you can and should implement best practices that streamline processes and reduce the company's risk, making it a safe and nourishing place to work. Doing so just makes good business sense. And it will set you apart from many of your competitors.

As an HR specialist, I can walk into a company and know right away whether it has good HR management in place. Without it, the work environment often shows negligence or lack of thought regarding safety. No honest-and-real conversations are taking place. There are more workplace accidents and a significantly higher risk of discrimination cases, even when unintentional. Without a good HR plan in place, and without being honest and real, a company will have higher turnover, so money is constantly being spent on training and recruiting. This constant training and recruiting turns into a spiral, which leads to higher rates for the company's unemployment insurance as well. These environments may very well have led to "The Great Resignation" because people are tired and they're seeking more.

There are strategies that will help you manage your HR responsibility *right now*. I'll teach you how to protect yourself against unnecessary risk and exposure so you can continue to focus on your other job responsibilities — like running the company or strutting your stuff when it comes to your functional expertise. I hope you'll find that honest-and-real HR is a useful tool, helping you to conduct business in an honest, respectful, and responsible work environment.

The great secret of quality HR management is that when your employees are happy and safe, you get an increase in productivity, an increase in your bottom line, and a reduction in incidents, disruptions, and turnover.

The great secret of quality HR management is that when your employees are happy and safe, you get an increase in productivity, an increase in your bottom line, and a reduction in incidents, disruptions, and turnover. (Granted, there is no controlling a global disruption like a pandemic, but there are disruptions you can prevent. And the more disruptions you can avoid, the smoother the business will run.) People want to work in an efficient organization where they are respected, where they respect others, and where everyone does their job. And when you do need to find someone new to cover a vacant position, these best practices are what will lead you to a fantastic new hire.

When you feel the thrill of finding an excellent new employee and get to watch this person grow and succeed (helping ignite additional growth and success for your company as well), I think that you might just find a little love in your heart for human resources after all. It's certainly my goal that you do.

A Global Disruption

At the start of 2020, the world as we once knew it came to a halt. News spread about a virus called the novel coronavirus (SARS-CoV-2) and, in no time flat, the virus itself was spreading. By February, it was in the United States, sickening people with an illness we came to know as COVID-19. Within days, the healthcare crisis became a human resources crisis and an economic one as well. A global pandemic was declared by the World Health Organization on March 11, 2020, and the crisis specifically and significantly impacted businesses and human resources operations on March 13, 2020, when the President of the United States announced a national emergency, basically shutting down almost everything in our society.

I remember it well, including the discussions we were having with clients leading up to that fateful and unexpected day. In one specific situation, a client had decided on March 12 that we were going to have a "practice" work-from-home day the following week for the entire organization of about 37 employees. Stay with me and I'll explain why this particular situation really stands out in my mind. We talked through the logistics of what that would have to look like, who would be responsible for which activities, and how we would communicate to the entire staff.

On Friday, March 13, 2020, we announced to the entire organization: "When you leave work today, take home whatever equipment and office supplies you will need for the next two (2) weeks." We were so sure that would be enough — that everyone would be back to work and life would continue as normal after a 14-day national quarantine. Two weeks seems so ridiculous (almost comical) now! Oh, if we had only known.

So why does this particular client stand out in my mind? Before COVID (pre-C, as we call it at my company now), employees had to choose one of three schedules. They could start work each weekday morning at 7:30, 8:00, or 8:30. That was it — you worked in the office during your designated hours, you took a very specific lunch break, and you left the office at a predetermined time each day. END OF STORY. You did not work from home, and you had to live in the Harrisburg, Pennsylvania, market except under a few very specific exceptions. Again, END OF STORY.

Today? Wow — a complete 180-degree turn. They will never be fully back in the office together — except under a very few exceptions. As to where an employee lives? It doesn't matter any longer ... as long as the employee's residence is in the Commonwealth of PA (the constituency they serve.)

Talk about a complete and total culture makeover. It was amazing to watch and an awesome experience to help develop. That's a success story if I've ever heard one!

Let's turn back to March 13, 2020. New terms became common language — "essential business," "pandemic," "first responders," "frontline workers," "flattening the curve," to name just a few. Regulatory agencies that we rarely dealt with in HR (pre-2020) became common references: the Department of Health and Human Services (HHS) and the Centers for Disease Control (CDC).

Both agencies had been around since 1953 and 1946 respectively. I remember, vaguely, the mention of both agencies earlier in my career but, frankly, I never referenced them or turned to them for guidance until 2020 — now they are bookmarked as "favorites." Human resources managers and our counterparts in companies without HR departments took on a whole new set of tasks — and I'm still kicking and screaming about some of them.

Suddenly, HR people were mired in discussions about the following (and so much more):

- I'm closed by government order — how can I pay the bills of the business if we're not generating revenue?

- I believe I'm an essential employer, but the government doesn't. *(Aren't all employers essential?)*

- I am an essential employer, the government says so, but I have some employees who are afraid to come to work.

- How do I pay my employees? Who has that much extra money lying around to pay people who aren't working while no money is coming into the business?

- My employee chose to go out of state (or country!) during a pandemic, and I don't want them back at work exposing everyone if they're carrying the virus.

- Do I take temperatures of my employees, or do I trust them to self-monitor?

- What do I do with someone who has a scratchy throat? Or a cough? What about when I know it's allergy season?

- Is it the company's fault if someone catches COVID-19 at work?

I could keep going and going; in fact, years later (this book is releasing in the spring of 2022), we're still coming up with new questions that never had to be faced before as an employer or as a nation.

For the first time I can remember (I was not here for the 1918 flu outbreak!), the United States government stepped up and to assist employers and employees in big ways. The feds offered significant support, particularly to small employers, by instituting the Family First Coronavirus Response Act ("FFCRA"), which spelled out very clear conditions in which some employers could receive reimbursement for paying their employees to miss work. This enabled employers to assist employees in human and compassionate ways (ways that were honest and real!), with minimal damage to the business's bottom line ... which was already being decimated by business conditions (unless you were a toilet-paper or plexiglass manufacturer!). Other ways of helping included the Coronavirus Aid, Relief, and Economic Security (CARES) Act which, among other things, required virus diagnostic testing to be covered by insurance companies. The Small Business Administration (SBA) jumped in as well with the Paycheck Protection Program (PPP). Businesses also gained insight into an SBA program that already existed: the Economic Injury Disaster Loan (EIDL).

The "new" agencies that we became acquainted with (DOH, CDC,) as well as our good-old standby (the Department of Labor), quickly assembled Frequently Asked Questions pages that were continually updated. Frankly, I am impressed by the speed with which they responded. Sure, it seemed slow while we were living through those painful first two weeks but, in retrospect, they moved the government wheel very quickly in the grand scale of things. For the first time in my career, I witnessed the HR impact of a national crisis (and that nation's response to the crisis). Nothing else had ever compared (not 9/11, not the 2008 recession). As HR leaders, we were — in many ways — on our own sort of "front line," trying to keep businesses and communities and small economies thriving.

On the opposite side of that "fast-moving" wheel, unemployment compensation bureaus were overwhelmed and understaffed nationally. No one was prepared for such an influx of eligible people. When the federal government did come to the rescue of the state bureaus, individual workers and their families were rescued (sometimes in big ways, especially in states where some people collecting unemployment enjoyed several months cashing checks that were larger than their original paychecks). The jury is still out on whether those unemployment supplements helped or hurt. Many people believed that the use of federal funds to overfund unemployment in every state might have unintentionally kept people from seeking new employment and returning to work in the short term.

Introducing Work/Life Balance: Important Lessons from a Global Pandemic

So, why didn't employees return to work in droves? Because they'd had unprecedented experiences and mindset shifts and a chance to reprioritize work, life, health, leisure, and family. One of the best things I witnessed during the onset of the pandemic was the number of families *outside* doing things *together*. (Who else could you hang with but the people you were quarantined with, right?!) Suddenly, people were picnicking in the front yard with their kids and exploring their neighborhoods on foot or bicycle or skateboard. It appeared that the entire world had s-l-o-w-e-d down. Many families learned to be families again; people had been forced to reevaluate their entire lives. Was work more important or was spending time with family more important? (And if you're wondering where

I stand on this, I happen to think that if you have a job and you have a family, attending to both is important.) In 2020-2021, we were all forced to learn to live differently and with less. Even those of us who were blessed to work (or receive pay) through the entire pandemic learned to live with less because a world in shutdown was offering so much less for us to consume or experience.

Companies learned to do with less also; those of us responsible for the operations of our organizations spent the time focusing on processes. Those companies that "pivoted" (oh, how I despise that word today) learned to survive (and, in some cases, thrive). Why would families/employees be any different? Restaurants learned to deliver their food at curbsides and via delivery drivers, consumers learned to experience the world differently, and employees began to rethink everything — about where they worked, how they worked, or whether they worked at all.

Remember my first company example — the client with the complete 180-degree turn from strict office hours to "meh, please just get your job done?" They're a common example of how organizational cultures can turn on a dime, especially when they're forced to do so. I've been blessed to witness many great cultural changes in the past two years. What I saw and what I was inspired by? Oh, so much.

The good stuff:

- Empathy as a corporate value
- Employees *can* be trusted to work from home
- Who cares when the work gets done as long as it gets done by the deadline?
- Bandwidth is important (both computer and personal)

- Technology as a way to connect at a human level (I should have bought stock in an online meeting platform)
- Our lives (at work and at home) changed irrevocably, in ways that were refreshing and healthy.

The not-so-good stuff:

- We missed *two* years of work (and life), sort of
- Online meetings tended to be exhausting, back-to-back, and sometimes time-wasting
- Loss of collaboration and office camaraderie among teams that didn't already have remote-work skills and a culture of keeping people close, despite geography
- Loss of connection to the people we know and to other human beings in general
- Our lives (work and home) changed unexpectedly, in ways that were shocking and scary and sometimes painful.

Human resources professionals played a huge part at the onset of the pandemic and will have an even bigger impact as we move into our future. *Your* involvement — either directly in HR or as an Accidental HR™ manager — will play a bigger role in the business forever. I encourage you to embrace this; do not run from it. It's scary — there are still too many unknowns and we're still traumatized from having our worlds so utterly rocked. We know the next crisis will come because this one taught us to "expect the unexpected." And now we can.

Be strong, be positive, and — most of all — keep the "human" in human resources. You are a person ... as are all your coworkers (your "internal" customers). Recognizing that truth may be the single best thing that came out of our universal battle with the Novel

Coronavirus outbreak. Be honest. Be real. Doing so makes you optimally resilient in the face of the most difficult challenges of all.

Throughout this book, as we discuss everyday HR operations, we'll also discuss how a business disruption might impact those processes, policies, and activities. We're now "crisis-aware" and disruption-focused ... and so are the lessons in this book.

Part One
The Proper Setup

Chapter One
What You Don't Know Can Hurt You

If you have even one employee on your payroll, you may be subject to federal, state, and local employment laws. Do you know if you're in compliance with the law? If one of the many local, state, or federal agencies comes knocking on your door, do you know how to protect yourself? Is your paperwork in order? Do you even *have* paperwork? There are things you need to know *right now* to make sure you're in compliance with the law. You don't want to risk becoming embroiled in a lengthy court case that could have been prevented by having the proper practices and documentation in place.

Federal Regulations

Table 1 is a good reference chart for the typical federal regulations that apply to companies with employee headcounts of particular sizes. As soon as you have one employee, full-time or part-time, there are more than 10 federal employment laws that you're responsible for.

If you've grown large enough to hire an employee, you've grown large enough to need an HR manager. If your company's not large, that person is *you*!

TABLE 1. FEDERAL REGULATIONS BY HEADCOUNT

These are the federal regulations that employers may be responsible for when they reach the listed employee count. Although this chart is focused on federal regulations, don't forget to check what state and local regulations may apply to employers with one or more employees.

Number of Employees	Regulation/Statute
1	Affordable Care Act (ACA)
	Drug-Free Workplace Act
	Employee Retirement Income Security Act (ERISA)
	Equal Pay Act
	Fair Credit Reporting Act (FCR)
	Fair Labor Standards Act (FLSA)
	Federal Unemployment Tax Act (FUTA)
	Federal Workers Compensation Laws
	Immigration Reform and Control Act (ICRA)
	National Labor Relations Act (NLRA)
	Occupational Safety and Health Administration (OSHA) Regulations
	Privacy Laws
	Uniformed Services Employment and Reemployment Rights Act (USERRA)
10	OSHA Record Keeping
15	Americans with Disabilities Act as Amended (ADAAA)
	Title VII of the Civil Rights Act
20	Age Discrimination in Employment Act (ADEA)
	Consolidated Omnibus Budget Reconciliation Act (COBRA)

(continued)

Number of Employees	Regulation/Statute
50	Affirmative Action Program
	Family and Medical Leave Act (FMLA)
100	EEO-1 Report and EEO-1, Component 2 Report
	Worker Adjustment and Retraining Notification Act (WARN)

As you add more employees to your workforce, you add more complexity to your HR management, more interpersonal issues, and more employment regulations. As an owner, you bear responsibility for the pressure that increases as you accept the responsibility of providing for more and more people. The money they earn working for you is their livelihood, and it gives them the ability to support their families. The work they do for you can add meaning and purpose to their lives. In turn, you promise to adhere to the regulations that were put in place to protect them. And it's not just the right thing or the "required" thing to do — smart HR practices make your job easier and your company more successful. Being honest and real through adherence to these regulations truly does help to ensure a safe, productive, and drama-free workplace for your employees and for you.

As you add more employees to your workforce, you add more complexity to your HR management, more interpersonal issues, and more employment regulations.

It helps to remember that these regulations weren't put in place to punish employers; they were put in place to *protect employees*. If you can make that switch in your brain, it will make following the regulations a whole lot easier. Even if a regulation seems arbitrary or arcane, each regulation has come about because, once upon a time, someone did something bad that caused that someone to hurt (physically, emotionally, financially) themselves or someone else. To prevent that injury or injustice from happening again, a protective regulation was created and is now enforced.

In my experience, the well-being and safety of employees is at the top of the list of importance for nearly every CEO or business owner. Employers are much more likely to wake up at night in a sweat, saying, "I have to make a payroll" than they are to wake up saying, "I have to make a profit." When you worry about payroll, you're showing that you care about the people who work for you and not just about increasing your profits. Learning about and following the necessary regulations is another way that you can demonstrate true care and consideration for your employees.

State Regulations

Each state has its own set of rules and regulations. It's up to you to familiarize yourself with the regulations for the state or states where your company does business. Many professionals believe my home Commonwealth of Pennsylvania has some of the strictest regulations in the nation, so what goes for Pennsylvania is usually a good high-water mark for the rest of the states, with one exception: California. California is a human resources world unto itself, with so many employee regulations that I can't even give you the number. In fact, both the Society for Human Resource Management (SHRM) and the HR Certification Institute (HRCI) offer special certifications just for California HR professionals. I will be honest and real here: other states are implementing specific regulations. California may not be alone much longer. Please do your homework.

With so many rules and regulations to keep track of, it's hard to know which to follow first: Does local override federal? Does state come before local? Instead of wading through a swamp of guesswork, simply follow the strictest authority. While federal regulations apply to all the states, you may also be subject to a stricter local or state regulations.

For example, if the city of San Francisco has a stricter definition of protected classes than the state of California (which already has a stricter definition of protected classes than the federal government), then employers in San Francisco need to follow the city regulations first. Even if you make a mistake, the agencies are going to work with you (rather than against you) if you've made your best attempt at a good-faith effort to follow the law.

The Agencies

In this section, I'll give you an overview of several regulatory agencies, including who they are, what they do, why they might come knocking on your door, and what you can do to minimize your risk of being out of compliance. First, however, there are three things that can help reduce your exposure regardless of the agency you're dealing with.

1. **Document everything.** The phrase you hear in real estate is "location, location, location." In human resources, it's "document, document, document." You don't need to put a detailed note into the employee file every time you have a conversation about X, Y, or Z, but by keeping accurate, timely, and consistent notes and records, you're going to minimize your risk in any situation and make life a whole lot easier for everyone. You don't need to be fancy — notes can be easily stored on your calendar or in your work log or day planner. Some people prefer to send themselves an e-mail. Even a simple note (for example, "Talked to Karen about overtime today") becomes stored and date stamped. Two years from now, when someone's looking for proof to back up

a claim, you'll be able to say, "Oh, yes, Mr. Investigator, here's my note. We had a conversation about this 08/19/2019." Proper documentation is a game changer.

2. **Expend effort and stay honest.** Making a good-faith effort and being real and honest will serve you well as you work with the various agencies, even if you make mistakes. For example, you can call the Occupational Safety and Health Administration (OSHA), enter a voluntary program with them, and, in turn, be protected from citations for a period of time. The agencies want to help you. I have an investigator with the Pennsylvania Department of Labor and Industry who I'll call before acting when I'm not sure of something regarding wages or hours. Time and again, he's told me that advice is free; it's the errors that are costly. Do yourself a favor and "measure twice, cut once."

3. **Get even closer to these agencies during times of local or national disruption.** Do not undercut any of these agencies as a resource during an emergency. At the end of the day, they're each here to help us maintain a working environment that is safe, fair, equitable, and harmless. During the early weeks and months of the Novel Coronavirus outbreak in 2020, many of these agencies rose to the occasion and provided excellent and timely guidance for employers and employees.

1. Occupational Safety and Health Administration (OSHA)

www.OSHA.gov

OSHA's job is to ensure that every employee is guaranteed a safe work environment, and OSHA's goal is to help employers have safe workplaces. OSHA's job is *not* to shake you down! If you don't have a safe workplace environment, it's OSHA's job to help you correct it. The premise of the law is to protect employees, and that's why OSHA is there.

Every employer has to follow OSHA's General Duty Clause. You can go to OSHA's website and read the full document, but the basic premise of the General Duty Clause is that an employer has a responsibility to provide a workplace that is "free from recognized hazards" that could cause harm.[1] That means it's your *duty* as employers to send your employees home whole and healthy, the same way they came to you when they were hired or when they started the day's shift.

If an employee gets hurt on the job, you're responsible. I like to explain it this way: If someone gets hurt in my house, I'm responsible for taking care of them. It seems like a no-brainer, but, time and again, negligence, a lack of time, or poor planning creates a situation that results in injury. Be honest, be real, "own" it. (That's why you have insurance.)

Why They Might Cause Drama

When OSHA visits, they will come for a few reasons. For now, let's look at the two most common: complaints and targeted industries (those with higher-than-normal hazards).

When OSHA receives an employee complaint, that complaint will remain anonymous. With small employers, oftentimes the complaint is difficult to keep truly anonymous. Imagine this scenario: You didn't train your workers to properly lock up the saw blade, and

---

[1] United States Department of Labor. "Sec. 5 Duties." https://www.osha.gov/laws-regs/oshact/section5-duties.

Kevin's finger got cut off. He's sitting there with a bandage; you never filed the accident with your insurance company *and* you forgot to pay his surgical bill. An OSHA official is standing there, clipboard in hand, asking you about it. You can safely bet that the complaint came from Kevin. But in larger companies, complaints are easier to keep anonymous, which encourages workers to reach out to OSHA if they've already reached out to you, but the safety hazard (or perceived safety hazard) remains.

Another reason OSHA might come to visit is that certain industries are more dangerous than others, and OSHA focuses on them with laser-like precision. For example, physicians' offices have a lot of "sharps" or needles. That's a specific hazard, and it makes sense for OSHA to target recognized businesses and industries that contain recognized hazards. If we step back and look at why they operate this way, it makes sense to target hazards rather than just blanket the entire world of industry and business with random spot-checks. It's easier (and more sensible) for OSHA to target hazards and focus on inspecting locations that likely contain those hazards.

Other industries with more hazards than average include trucking, transportation, and industries that use heavy machinery or dangerous items like meat cutters — anything that could easily hurt people, even by mistake.

It's your right to refuse OSHA entry, as your business is private property. But if you look at the big picture and take human nature into consideration, it's better to let them in so they can do their job rather than irritate them and make them suspicious. It is your right to turn them away; however, I don't recommend it. They'll just come back irritated and holding a warrant. Now, instead of just looking at the blocked fire exit they were originally there to investigate, they'll look at *everything*.

It *is* acceptable to say, "I'm sorry, the person you need to speak with isn't available right now." If your office manager is responsible for your record keeping and safety notes, it's perfectly acceptable to say, "Our office manager is not available right now. He'll be back tomorrow. Can we schedule a time for you to meet with him?" Most likely, they're going to agree to wait, depending on the severity of the complaint. They don't want to set you up to fail. OSHA's goal is simply to correct any problems and to ensure a safe workplace for employees.

Minimizing Your Risk and Exposure by Being Honest and Real

There are safety hazards in *every* environment. It drives me insane when I walk past an unattended file cabinet with an open drawer. Several things could occur: It could tip on you. You could walk into it. You could scrape your arm on the metal. It's a common hazard, yet it's so simple to close the file drawer and remove that hazard. Be aware of your environment, and help your employees do the same. Awareness is the key point of any safety program.

If your employees have a complaint, it's incumbent upon you to honestly listen to what they have to say. For example, if they're constantly saying, "The back door sticks so badly — I always have to go out the side way," then go find out why, and fix the door. Be aware of your environment.

Housekeeping makes a difference, so tidy up! You can't walk into a box in the hallway, if there's no box in the hallway.

Beyond the General Duty Clause, which activates when you have one or more employees, you may have to maintain certain statistical records of accidents once you have 10 or more employees. The OSHA 300 log needs to be maintained "live" throughout the year to record any workplace accidents that occur. Each year, between

February and April, you must post a summary of any accidents, or report if there are none. Generally, the summaries should be posted in a conspicuous location where employees will see them — perhaps in the same location as your required federal and state law postings. (We have no affiliation with them, but highly recommend www.allinoneposters.com as the least expensive site for the purchase of required employment posters.)

Once you have 10 or more employees, if OSHA visits, they will immediately request your current OSHA logs plus your logs for the previous five years. If you have them at the ready, you're ahead of the game, so don't be lax with yourself on this point. Having that log up to date helps OSHA and protects you.

2. U.S. Department of Labor (DOL)

www.DOL.gov

The DOL is responsible for many of the regulations you will deal with, including the Fair Labor Standards Act (FLSA), child labor laws, and the Consolidated Omnibus Budget Reconciliation Act (COBRA).

Consolidated Omnibus Budget Reconciliation Act (COBRA)

COBRA is the requirement to provide temporary continuous healthcare for your covered employees, their spouses, former spouses, and dependent children once group health coverage is lost due to resignation, termination, or reduction in hours. *You are responsible for COBRA if you have 20 or more employees and you offer healthcare.* COBRA requires specific notices and deadlines, so pay close attention to the regulations, and consult a professional. Many states have enacted what's called "mini-COBRA" for businesses with fewer than twenty employees.

Uniformed Services Employment and Reemployment Rights Act (USERRA)

The DOL is also responsible for enforcement of the Uniformed Services Employment and Reemployment Rights Act (USERRA). USERRA provides protection for our uniformed service personnel when they're deployed and reemployment provisions for when they return.

If an employee (who is also a member of the uniformed services) is deployed, the employer must release that person to go on deployment. Upon returning, that employee has a specific number of days to go to the employer and say, "I want my job back." This is the one thing that is *not* the employer's responsibility to track. It is the uniformed service employee's responsibility to come back within the specified time frame, which is determined by the length of the deployment. If the employee comes back within that time frame, you must give the job back to them with the same seniority, pay, status, and other benefits determined by seniority.

What Small Business Owners Need to Know

This measure serves as a protection for employees serving in the armed forces. Small businesses must know about and prepare for the possibility of military deployments for their employees because there are potential consequences to such departures. For example, say that your employee is deployed for one year, and you've had to fill the position in the meantime. The "replacement" is now integrated into your business and relies on you, so it could be hard to let the "replacement" go. Ideally, you'll have a plan in place to integrate them into another position, or written communication clearly stating the position is temporary. Once your uniformed services employee requests their job back, the USERRA requires you to reinstate them as though they were never gone.

Exempt or Non-Exempt

The DOL also monitors workers' statuses as *exempt* or *non-exempt* employees. While the specifics of this topic are complicated and changing rapidly, the basic premise of exempt and non-exempt will stay the same.

Exempt employees are ineligible for overtime pay and are generally salaried workers. Non-exempt employees are entitled to earn overtime and are generally hourly workers. Under this classification system, an exempt person is paid the same for a 60-hour workweek as they are for a 30-hour workweek. A non-exempt person's weekly earnings change based on the actual number of hours that they have worked.

HR Insider Tip: Calculating Overtime

Overtime is generally based on a standard of 40-hour workweeks. If a non-exempt employee works more than that, they must be paid overtime of at least 1.5 times their regular wage. In most circumstances, employers are not required to count vacations, holidays, or sick days when calculating overtime. For the purposes of overtime, a workweek must be defined as a period of seven consecutive days. However, the employer could publish the workweek from Monday through Sunday or Saturday through Friday, no matter what the pay cycle is. Don't forget to double-check your state and local wage and hour laws as well.

Exemption status is based upon a job's *duties*, regardless of the job title or pay. Weekly earnings are the first exemption test described in the Fair Labor Standards Act, but what it ultimately comes down to are the duties of the position and how much discretion and independent judgment in matters of significance goes with the job. Your definition of *independent judgment* probably isn't the same as the DOL's, so there are checklists out there that can help you determine if a position should be exempt or non-exempt. If you don't get the answer you want from the checklist, then you might need to modify the job description or *manage the employee's schedule to reduce or eliminate overtime.* Have an honest- and- real conversation with the employee before just cutting their hours — help them understand the reason for the change.

Why They Might Cause Drama

Wage Complaints: Most commonly, the DOL knocks on your door because of a wage complaint. Perhaps, you didn't pay overtime properly.

Child Labor Laws: You may have minors working for you and find the child labor law people on your doorstep (child labor also falls under the DOL's umbrella).

Misclassification: Employee or Independent Contractor: The DOL may show up because of an employee/contractor (contracted freelancer) misclassification. The DOL continues to hire additional investigators simply to look at misclassification issues, which are generally brought to light in one of two ways. One way is through unemployment claims. When an independent contractor files for unemployment after their job is done, the employer responds to the claim by stating that the person was an independent contractor, not an employee. However, through the unemployment process, it may be determined that the contracted worker should have been classified as an employee. The other main source of misclassification issues is when an independent contractor gets hurt on the job. As an independent contractor, they are not covered by your workers' compensation insurance policy. However, the workers' compensation process may result in a determination that the individual was technically an employee.

> **HR Insider Tip: Start with the IRS Guidelines**
>
> I always recommend that employers start with the IRS guidelines as an initial guide to determine if they are classifying their workers correctly. The IRS provides an excellent form that can help you make an informed determination — it's called Form SS-8. If you're still not sure after answering the questions on the form, you can actually submit the form to the IRS for a formal determination.[2] Of course, as with most employment law questions, you should seek the advice of knowledgeable counsel, as federal and state wage and hour laws are complex and often depend on the specifics of very particular circumstances.

Minimizing Your Risk and Exposure by Being Honest and Real

The DOL is there to protect the rights of the workers under your care. They simply want to make sure that people are being paid properly and treated fairly. If you are being proactive and staying on top of things, you can ensure a great relationship with the DOL.

Document your decision-making process and reasoning. This step is key to minimizing your risk with every agency. If you can back up what you're saying with documentation, it's going to make life a whole lot easier for everyone.

---

2 Income Tax Witholding. http://www.irs.gov/pub/irs-pdf/fss8.pdf.

Ensure that your employees and independent contractors (if any) are properly classified. If workers are independent contractors, treat them as such. Ideally, they will have their own business and will perform services for other businesses, not just your company. In addition, don't supply them with equipment, don't set their hours, and don't tell them what to do. If you want to direct the work they do, put them on your payroll. With contracted employees, I don't care how many hours they work. I pay the invoice for the services per the contract. You're paying them for the *service*, not for their time.

Follow the rules when you hire minors. The rules are very specific, so be mindful of them.

Honestly listen to your employees. If an employee comes to you and says, "I think I should be making overtime," they have probably done some homework. It would be wise to take a closer look. Be thankful that they came to you instead of going to an outside agency.

Honestly listen to your employees.

Be consistent. To everyone, all the time. Don't set yourself up for a complaint by playing favorites or by letting certain employees get under your skin.

---

3. Equal Employment Opportunity Commission (EEOC)

www.EEOC.gov

The EEOC is responsible for enforcement of Title VII of the Civil Rights Act of 1964, as amended, and other federal, anti-discrimination laws. It ensures that employers don't discriminate based on race, creed, color, national origin, sex, religion, and several other protected classifications. The federal anti-discrimination laws also prohibit retaliation against an individual who complains of unlawful discrimination or other protected activity. Recently, the EEOC also prohibited discrimination based on sexual orientation. The EEOC prohibits discrimination in hiring, firing, wages, and terms and conditions of employment.

As America becomes more diverse, it also becomes more confusing. Simply put, if something has no bearing on an individual's ability to do the job, then look past it (even if you don't understand it). How in the world would a long beard or a butterfly tattoo on the inside of the wrist prohibit or prevent against someone answering customer service phone calls? It just wouldn't.

When it comes to adhering to the EEOC's rules, there are a million what-ifs, but the real truth of the matter comes down to whether something affects an employee's ability to do the job. Does a religious headscarf prevent someone from serving a cupcake? No. Neither does a wheelchair. Neither does an individual's pronouns, skin color, or genetics.

Be honest; be real. You don't have to understand where someone is coming from, but you do have to respect their background. Your job is to have the best-qualified people to do the work of your organization, period.

When it comes to adhering to the EEOC's rules, there are a million what-ifs, but the real truth of the matter comes down to whether something affects an employee's ability *to do the job.*

Many people panic when faced with something that might look like discrimination because they're afraid they'll be sued. If you've kept good records of job-related reasons for your actions, then it's easy to be confident in defending your actions. It's not religious discrimination to terminate an employee because they can't work the mandated schedule for employees in a job classification, even if that scheduling conflict arises because they've decided to start attending religious services more regularly. Make decisions based upon the job-related needs of the business, *not* the circumstances of the individual. Be honest with the employee about the reason you've made the decision.

It's wise to stop, think, and make sure that you're on the level, but don't let fear prevent you from taking care of your business.

Why They Might Cause Drama

There are two different kinds of discrimination that the EEOC is looking for: *disparate treatment* and *disparate impact*. Disparate treatment discriminates against an individual. Disparate impact discriminates against a group of protected individuals. If it's proven that minorities can't score as well as white people on the test because of the way it's written, then the test has a disparate impact on minorities.

The EEOC also responds to complaints of *unlawful harassment*. Most people immediately think of sexual harassment, but unlawful harassment also applies to any protected classification. It can be confusing. For example, a headscarf may be protected, but a nose ring is likely not, because the two objects do not represent the same value in that person's life. The head covering is likely for religious reasons and is therefore protected, but nose rings don't typically fall into a protected class. You may also hear from the EEOC if you fail to reasonably accommodate employees so they can continue to perform the essential functions of their job due to illness or disability.

In diversity and harassment training, which is a great way to reduce the risk of litigation and foster a productive workplace, the key word is *respect*. I don't have to agree with my coworkers' religious beliefs, but I have a responsibility to respect that it's their right to believe what they want, just as I expect them to respect my faith or lack thereof. I don't have to understand it, I don't have to agree with it, I don't have to accept it, and I don't have to follow it, but I *do* have to respect it.

The key word is *respect*.

As our world continues to advance and our employees and society in general become more vocal about the need for inclusion, some of your staff may struggle with understanding someone's use of pronouns. Talk to your employees honestly — someone's chosen pronouns are to be respected and not questioned. Whether Taylor uses she/her, he/him, or they/them pronouns has absolutely no bearing on Taylor's ability to do the job. And don't forget to have honest conversations with customers/clients on this topic, where possible. No client should be chiming in with "Sorry, but you look like a woman to me" or calling Bree by she/her pronouns if Bree or others in your organization have clearly introduced they/them pronouns for Bree. You have a responsibility to protect your entire staff from mistreatment during the exercise of their job duties, even when such mistreatment comes from outside your organization.

Minimizing Your Risk and Exposure by Being Honest and Real

As a leader, you set the tone for a respectful workplace by the way you treat your employees and by the expectations you clearly set in place regarding how they should treat each other.

Train your employees. The best way to minimize exposure is to help your employees understand and be able to define protected, unlawful harassment or discrimination. Implementing anti-harassment, discrimination, and retaliation policies and conducting anti-discrimination, harassment, and diversity training is a good start to reduce your risk of complaints. As strange as it may seem, bullying is probably not harassment. It is most likely unacceptable under the policies of the company and is probably a violation of work rules, but it doesn't necessarily cross the line into unlawful harassment if it is not based on the person's gender, religion, national origin, or other protected classification. Bullying must be connected to a protected class before it becomes unlawful harassment.

Implementing anti-harassment, discrimination, and retaliation policies and conducting anti-discrimination, harassment, and diversity training is a good start to reduce your risk of complaints.

Let me offer two examples to illustrate the difference. Super-Sales-Person John (SSP John) is a bully.

> ***Example One:*** SSP John yells; no one likes working with him. He yells at everyone regardless of their age, race, creed, color ... SSP John just likes to yell (at anyone/everyone except his customers

who ADORE him). SSP John is a bully and acting inappropriately. SSP John needs a talking to!

Example Two: SSP John yells at the longer-term customer service staff (i.e., older staff) because they don't respond to his texts; they follow company policy. SSP John yells and yells and yells at them. SSP John buys gifts for the newer reps (i.e., younger staff) because they always respond to his texts. SSP John is a bully, acting inappropriately and could possibly get the company involved in an age discrimination case. SSP John needs an honest-and-real talking to!

Document, document, document. Follow your policies and procedures. Investigate promptly and thoroughly. If you have a discrimination complaint, you're going to want to be able to show that everything that happens in your business — hiring, firing, promotions, and disciplinary actions — happens based on merit and ability, not because of favoritism or prejudice.

3A. Americans with Disabilities Act as Amended (ADA/ADAAA)

www.ADA.gov

The Americans with Disabilities Act (ADA), as amended, protects individuals with known and perceived disabilities. The ADA Amendments Act of 2008 (ADAAA) greatly expanded the ADA's definition of *disability*.

Suppose someone walks in on crutches to apply for a job, and I say to my HR coordinator, "I wonder what her problem is." I have potentially protected that person under the ADAAA because I have perceived her as having a disability.

That said, you shouldn't be afraid of the ADAAA. Employers fear that once employees tell them they have disabilities, they'll never be able to fire them, even if they have performance issues. That's just not true. Disability or no disability, employers are allowed to expect a certain level of performance from their employees. The essential functions of the job must be completed, with or without accommodation.

As soon as someone says, "I have a disability," it's the responsibility of the employer to protect that employee (and the company) under the ADAAA. To do that, the employer and employee must enter into what's called the *interactive dialogue*. This is a process by which you lay out the expectations of the company, ask the employee what they are able to do and what accommodations they might need (as documented by a healthcare provider), and continue the dialogue regarding what is or is not a reasonable accommodation.

For example, if you have an outstanding receptionist who is starting to have difficulty hearing, you might first notice behaviors like calls being transferred to the wrong people and messages being mixed up. These issues are uncharacteristic for someone who's been a fantastic employee for years. After speaking to her and identifying the problem — hearing loss, not a performance issue — you have started the interactive process, allowing both the employee and the employer to identify the best ways to accommodate and ensure she may continue to perform her job confidently and successfully.

The solution may be to install a $50 adapter for the handset, which is a reasonable accommodation. But what if the adapter costs $5,000 and your entire phone system only cost $3,000? That may *not* be a reasonable accommodation. At that point, you need to explore other reasonable alternatives (which may include reassigning her to another job). Only after you explore all other reasonable options should you consider terminating this employee (and please consult with your attorney before making this decision on your own.)

There are *many* accommodations that we can and should consider. A leave of absence is often considered a reasonable accommodation, but that doesn't mean that when an employee requests a six-month leave that we must grant a leave for six months. You need someone doing that job, but before you make decisions, have the honest conversation and document everything you do or attempt to do to make it right. Don't set a hard line and terminate everyone after a set period of time is over.

Then we get into the whole Family and Medical Leave Act (FMLA) as well, but there's more on that later. For now, know that even a small company may need to consider an unpaid leave of absence for an employee with a serious illness.

The interactive process also protects *you*, the employer. If an employee has come in and said, "I have a hearing problem, but if you get me a headset, I won't have any more issues," the issues may, in fact, continue even after they are provided the headset. In that case, you may be dealing with a performance issue, not a disability issue, and can address it as such.

Minimizing Your Risk and Exposure by Being Honest and Real

Write thorough and accurate job descriptions. During hiring, you should always present the job description to the candidates and ask, "Are you able to perform the essential functions of the job with or without reasonable accommodation?" If they look at the job description and agree to it, take them at their word.

Don't guess at how you would or would not be able to perform the job in their shoes; have an honest-and-real conversation and determine if a reasonable accommodation is even needed or can be reached. If the candidate says, "I can't stand for eight hours, but I can do the job if I have a chair," then enter into a dialogue with them. You can agree to get them a chair or, if that's not possible, you can say, "There's no room for a chair in that area, so we can't provide a chair. Would a stool work?" You've attempted a valid offer of accommodation, and now it's up to the candidate to accept or decline.

You are not a doctor.* While it's our responsibility to comply with the ADAAA as soon as we learn that an employee has a disability or we "perceive it," it's also important to keep in mind, in an effort to protect the company, to not just grant an employee's requests without consulting a medical professional. If somebody tells you that medically, they need a different chair, then you want a medical professional to confirm that claim and give you guidance. The medical professional may tell you, "For this condition, you need a chair with task arms on it, but you don't need the $400 chair the employee is asking for." Again, you gain all this knowledge through the interactive dialogue.

Don't be afraid to get a second opinion. If your employee comes to you with medical documentation that seems too good to be true (i.e., potentially forged or written by a family member who just happens to be a physician), check it out. The employee may also be self-diagnosing an issue, so it's important to get a professional medical opinion.

In all of this, be proactive, and don't bend to fear or prejudice. And you may find that entering into that dialogue leads you to hiring or keeping a wonderful employee who you may previously have overlooked, not realizing how well they could perform the job.

---

* Well, maybe you actually *are* a qualified healthcare provider *and* the owner of the business. It may be wise, in these circumstances, to rely upon other healthcare providers to get you the confirmation you need to best manage the accommodation request.

4. U.S. Immigration and Customs Enforcement (ICE)

Formerly the U.S. Immigration and Naturalization Services (INS)

www.ICE.gov

U.S. Immigration and Customs Enforcement (ICE) falls under the Department of Homeland Security, whose primary mission is to promote homeland security and public safety. ICE focuses on "smart immigration enforcement."

ICE has been directly involved with all employers since its creation in 2003. An employer's interaction with ICE has to do with an individual's eligibility to work in the United States. It has nothing to do with their citizenship or their culture. We document proof of employment eligibility through the I-9 form.

> **An employer's interaction with ICE has to do with an individual's eligibility to work in the United States. It has nothing to do with their citizenship or their culture.**

Employers should always be sure they are using the most current I-9 form, so double-check the expiration date on the form. On the I-9, there's a section for the employee to complete and a section for the employer.

You should absolutely *not* ask if someone is an American citizen during a job interview. Instead, you should ask, "Are you eligible to work in the United States?" That is a perfectly acceptable question.

You do not need to be an American citizen to be eligible to work in the United States.

Similarly, you may *not* tell new hires what items they should present for identification. Instead of asking for their driver's license and Social Security card, provide them with the list of acceptable documents listed on the I-9. You *may* say, "Most people present their driver's license and Social Security card." (It's semantics, I know, but ...)

In my experience as a consultant, the I-9 is the largest record-keeping failure people make, simply because employees and employers don't fill out the form correctly. Filling out the I-9 improperly can cost an employer anywhere from $500 to $23,000 in civil fines and can involve criminal penalties ranging from a $3,000 fine to six months in jail.[3] However, mistakes on the I-9 are usually simple to avoid. The instructions for filling out the form are on the form itself.

In my experience as a consultant, the I-9 is the largest recordkeeping failure people make, simply because employees and employers don't fill out the form correctly.

The most common mistake made by both employees and employers filling out the I-9 is the date format. The second most common error is in the Employer Certification Section by forgetting to include the hire date (in proper date format). It's in the small print right above the employer signature section. To fill it out correctly, enter the date on which the employee started working; otherwise, it's a line-item fine, which may cost $230!

---

[3] U.S. Citizenship and Immigration Services. "Penalties." Last Reviewed/Updated: 07/10/2019. http://www.uscis.gov/i-9-central/penalties

Why They Might Cause Drama

An ICE audit is more of a record-keeping audit. Other agencies might come in and say, "I want to see a *sampling* of your record keeping. I want to see personnel files for five current employees and two terminated employees." ICE is different because they come in and say, "I want to see *all* your I-9s." They want everything.

> **In the days before your appointment with ICE, if you realize you've missed something on an I-9, you can and should correct it.**

Minimizing Your Risk and Exposure by Being Honest and Real

In addition to documenting everything, which is standard risk prevention for dealing with every agency, there are many things you can do to protect yourself.

Correct your mistakes. There's nothing wrong with you self-auditing your I-9s. I encourage you to do it, if needed, but to make sure you maintain a list of the errors that you discovered and the steps you took to correct those errors. *Document, document, document.* If ICE does come in, you can say, "We self-audited and found these errors. This is what we did to fix them." They'll appreciate the good-faith effort to correct any mistakes, but they'll expect you to have kept records of any changes.

When making corrections, never, ever use correction fluid or tape (e.g., Wite-Out) on an I-9. If you need to make a correction, use a single strike-through, and then date and initial the change. Remember, this is a legal, federal document.

If you decide that the whole I-9 form needs to be redone, do not destroy the original. Have the employee fill out a new form, and then attach the old form to the back of the new one. This demonstrates that the original document was filled out in the first 72 hours of employment, even if it was done improperly. Let ICE know that your audit revealed so many mistakes that your correction was to fill out a new form.

If you fail to fill out the form in the first 72 hours, don't try to back date. Similarly, don't back date new forms or corrections. Be honest. Make a true *good-faith effort* — that's the key phrase with all the agencies. If you're demonstrating a good-faith effort, they are less likely to attach punitive damages to any citations or fines.

Ask for help. It's perfectly reasonable to call and ask for help or clarification. Our office calls E-Verify — a federal government database used to confirm information on the I-9 — regularly. Federal contractors and some state contractors are required to use E-Verify.

Get familiar with filling out these simple forms. Make sure you're filling out every single line. Accuracy and completeness are critical; failure to specifically follow the instructions can be costly. This isn't something to gloss over or to pass off to an intern. This is serious business.

Filling out I-9 forms isn't something to gloss over or to pass off to an intern. This is serious business.

---

5. The National Labor Relations Board (NLRB) and the National Labor Relations Act (NRLA)

www.NLRB.gov

A common mis-perception is that the National Labor Relations Board (NLRB) deals only with union companies. That is a false assumption. The National Labor Relations Act (NLRA) covers nearly all employers, both union and union-free.

The NLRA protects an employee's right to concerted activity. That means that employees can discuss wages, terms, and conditions of employment with anyone at any time. If your employee handbook says, "You may not discuss your wages with any other employee," then you are violating the NLRA.

Social media brought the NLRA to everyone's attention. An employee was fired after posting nasty stuff about his employer on social media. Seems logical, right? The problem is that some of his coworkers chimed into the conversation, both agreeing and disagreeing. The minute coworkers entered that conversation, it became a protected, concerted activity. If none of his coworkers had chimed in and made this a "discussion of wages, terms and conditions or employment," his termination may have been able to stand.

Social media brought the NLRA to everyone's attention.

If someone is using social media to bash the company or complain about supervisors or coworkers, you can sit them down and have an honest and real conversation, "Do you think that was really the best way to address your problem?" But do not discipline that person for posting. What employees do on their own time is generally their business, even if it's complaining about work. After your talk, hopefully the employee will take it upon themself to take down the post and stop using social media as an outlet for work complaints.

The NLRA also addresses union elections and recognition of unions. While union membership is declining, elections and union recognition is a hot topic with this agency, and it always will be. The unions have a really, *really* large voice in Washington.

I've worked in both union and union-free environments, and there are advantages and disadvantages to both. I wholeheartedly believe there's less of a need today for union representation than ever before. In my experience, unions will promise the world to their dues-paying members, but the realities of economics are such that a company can only provide what the company can provide. If I can't afford, as a business owner, to provide 100 percent company-paid medical coverage, then I can't afford it, no matter what the union demands. And if I'm forced to offer something I can't afford, my only recourse may be to start laying people off or to close the business.

While you may not worry about an organizing campaign, you still need to be aware of this law, because the same rules apply: employees are allowed to congregate, they are allowed to discuss their wages, and they are allowed to discuss their work environment. And when they come to you, you're allowed to try to make things better, if you can.

Employees are allowed to congregate, they are allowed to discuss their wages, and they are allowed to discuss their work environment. And when they come to you, you're allowed to try to make things better, if you can.

Why They Might Cause Drama

If you've violated your employees' right to congregate or their right to put up information about a union meeting in the break room, chances are you'll be hearing from the NLRB. If your social media policy is too restrictive and/or you discipline employees for their activities on social media, you'll most likely hear from the NLRB.

Minimizing Your Risk and Exposure by Being Honest and Real

The best way to minimize your exposure is to make sure that you have a solid no-solicitation policy. But there's a compromise with that because "no solicitation" means *no solicitation*. So that means that you can't sell your daughter's Girl Scout cookies, just like the union can't pamphlet your workplace. Once you break your own rule, it's a free-for-all.

_____

Once you break your own rule, it's a free-for-all.

_____

Because it's nearly impossible to enforce a strict "nothing" policy, it's best to compromise. Let your employees sell the Girl Scout cookies in non-work areas like the break room during non-work time, but know that it opens the door for an employee to put up union information in the same area. Whether you approve or not, it's better to know what's coming in the front door than to force everyone to sneak through the back door.

6. Department of Transportation (DOT)
www.DOT.gov

If your business has any vehicles with a gross value weight (GVW) in excess of 10,000 pounds, they fall under certain Department of Transportation (DOT) regulations. At 26,001 pounds, a special license is required. For reference, a 10,001-pound vehicle could be something like a moving truck, and a 26,001-pound vehicle would be closer to a semi-truck. However, you need to consider every vehicle your business has — tractors, pickups, and so on.

Even if you only have vehicles under 10,000 pounds, you may still need to pay attention to DOT regulations. The setup that's most often overlooked is a pickup truck hauling a trailer with a piece of equipment on it. People tend to think of that setup as consisting of three separate items, but as soon as they're linked together and/or stacked, they need to be counted as one vehicle for weight purposes. For example, you may have a setup where the pickup truck's GVW is 6,000 pounds, the tractor's GVW is 3,000 pounds, and the piece of equipment on the trailer has a GVW of 2,000 pounds. You are now in excess of 10,000 pounds, and there are certain record-keeping requirements for the commercial motor vehicle operator (i.e., your driver).

Why They Might Cause Drama

If you don't have a DOT number or a number assigned by your local public utility commission, you're probably going to stay under the radar unless your driver is pulled over or involved in a crash. But a crash is the most common reason that DOT comes to your door. They may also become aware of your company through a roadside inspection, either at the weigh stations you pass on the highway or if your driver is pulled over for a traffic offense.

Minimizing Your Risk and Exposure by Being Honest and Real

Know your equipment. Find out how much it weighs (it's generally posted right inside the door of the vehicle). Make a list of the ways you combine equipment and find out how much those configurations weigh. Determine if your drivers need special licenses.

The very first level of record keeping includes a medical certification card for the driver, a copy of their driver's license, and their driving record in the form of a motor vehicles report (MVR). These are just a few of the required forms.

If you suspect that DOT requirements might pertain to you but you aren't sure, give them a call. They are there to help you, to protect your employees, and to assist you in following standards.

With all agencies, remember that an honest and good-faith effort goes a long way. If you're trying and you're open and honest with them, they'll work with you as you learn the various ins and outs of their requirements and regulations.

Your Employees – Why THEY Might Cause Drama

Okay — you're not allowed to laugh at the section title. I'm being serious. Indeed, drama-free HR requires keeping agencies from coming knocking on your door. But the agencies aren't the only ones who might cause drama or headaches. Your employees will cause HR-related drama that can be proactively avoided or mitigated through honest-and-real treatment, consideration, and conversations.

Those of us in "accidental HR" or in formal HR roles have heard it all. "Suzie looked at me funny." "Joe talks too loud." "Marie is a gossip." "Jerome never talks to me." "Betsy told Harry that Megan likes James." I'm sure you can name one or two that you wish you had *never* heard. Employees should never feel like they can't come talk to you, but let's be sure we give employees the tools they need to resolve their own issues — so they know what to do at work, how to do it, how they are expected to interact with each other, and how to communicate through difficult moments.

Minimizing Your Risk and Exposure by Being Honest and Real

You might be thinking, "Karen, what's the best way to reduce the drama from my employees?" Hands down and every time — *honest-and-real conversations.* My gosh, they can be tough to hold sometimes — especially if the topic is body odor, interpersonal relationships, or someone failing to meet your expectations. But aren't some of the best things in life a challenge worth working toward and achieving?

Lead by example when speaking with your staff. If you expect managers to have honest conversations with their employees, be sure you are being honest with your managers. Build accountability, trust, and respect in the organization. Establish a mission that speaks not just to your customers but to your employees as well. Develop and share core values that have meaning and that support the mission of the organization. Share your vision for the future and bring the team *with* you!

7. Our New Friends: Health and Human Services (HHS) and the Centers for Disease Control and Prevention (CDC)

www.HSS.gov
www.CDC.gov

While these agencies have been in existence since 1953 and 1946 respectively, they never played a big role with employers. Then COVID-19 entered our lives. To this day, I still reference the CDC site on a weekly basis as the result of a pandemic policy instituted by a client.

Health and Human Services, originally called the Department of Health, Education, and Welfare (HEW,) was enacted by Congress in 1953.[4] A variety of smaller agencies fall under HHS and, while they have a new name, they still have responsibility for such things as advances in science, public health, and many social agencies.

The CDC started in Atlanta in 1946 and has since become one of the HHS agencies.[5] Even before COVID, the CDC has been exploring and fighting diseases in the US and through consultation abroad with the focus of keeping the public healthy and strong. We can rest assured that there are epidemiologists, scientists, and staff behind the scenes working every day for us. Both groups are available to employers and employees alike. Moving forward, these agencies will play a big role in the development of health-and-safety initiatives and policies at work.

---

4   https://www.hhs.gov/about/historical-highlights/index.html

5   https://www.cdc.gov/about/history/index.html

So far, we've explored organizations and people that can create drama in your business. Now, let's move into the *systems* that can further minimize your risk and exposure with your employees (those pesky door knockers). Review the sections on setting up your HR, bringing employees on board, running the ship, and effectively parting ways. Keep this book handy. Dog-ear it; use Post-It notes and highlighters; write in the margins; keep it close to you and the drama will soon settle in to systems, processes, and procedures.

Chapter Two
Job Descriptions

Job descriptions are at the hub of the wheel of successful human resource management. Everything else you deal with comes out of job descriptions and works in concert to form a functioning unit. Lose one or two spokes, and you can hobble along. Lose the hub, and you're not going anywhere.

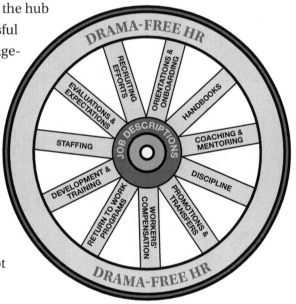

You can recruit all you want, but your recruiting won't be successful unless you know exactly what you're looking for. Going forward, unless new employees understand exactly what their responsibilities are, they will be slow to start-up and to provide value. Without solid job descriptions, your coaching and mentoring lose their focus — you may advocate one thing one day, and another thing the next. No one can be successful in an environment like that, and if you intend to discipline an employee for poor job performance, both of you need to have a deep understanding of the job's expectations. And if someone is leaving their position (even when retiring or being promoted) or if you have to terminate an individual, you want to fully understand the job responsibilities and what will be required to fulfill them.

The best way to create a job description is by determining the *essential functions* of a job. Essential functions are a lot more than just the tasks of the job; they are the basic reasons why the job exists.

The best way to create a job description is by determining the *essential functions* of a job. Essential functions are a lot more than just the tasks of the job; they are the basic reasons why the job exists. To capture those essential functions, a job description should be written much like a resume. For example, instead of saying, "Push the first button on the phone to answer an incoming call many times a day," you should say, "Answer heavy call volume." You should not get into the nitty-gritty of the actual *process* of the job, but you do want to describe the *overall* task or responsibility.

The Americans with Disabilities Act impacts job descriptions because when we talk about the interactive dialogue, we need to know the *essential functions* required. We also need to know what physical and work-environment exposures are involved.

To illustrate *essential functions*, let's go back to our example of a receptionist. The essential functions of the job — the primary reasons the job exists — are to greet guests when they come in and to answer incoming calls. There might be other secondary responsibilities or tasks that the person does — the receptionist might match accounts payables to purchase orders or stuff envelopes for mass mailings — but the *purpose* of that job is to greet visitors when they come in and answer incoming calls. It's that simple.

Now let's look at how a job description might interact with the ADAAA and accommodations. The essential function of the job of *forklift driver* is driving the forklift. A secondary responsibility might include refilling propane tanks and putting them on shelves in the garage. Maybe an applicant can drive a forklift, but he can't lift heavy gas cans. Technically, he is still a good candidate because he can fulfill the essential functions of the position. He can still fill the gas cans — we just need someone else to lift the cans.

An added feature that you can include in a job description is what's called *scope* — the depth and breadth of the position — such as how many people report to the position and the sales volume required of that position. Describe some of the quantitative aspects of the job. This helps you in hiring and allows applicants to make their own determinations about whether they're a good fit.

Another critical piece of information for the ADA is the *physical and work environment*. If the position requires sitting at a desk for an extended period of time while utilizing a computer and telephone, a healthcare provider can read into that and determine that the employee would need to be able to sit for long periods of time and that the employee will be using their arms, fingers, and forearms.

Again, the physical and work environment characteristics need to be clear in the job description to avoid complications should the need arise for an interactive dialogue. Having these characteristics in place makes a difference, even in cases where you're dealing with workers' compensation and return-to-work programs. It's much easier to get an individual back to work if you can present the evaluating physician with a solid job description that covers the responsibilities of the position and the work environment. It's also better for the doctor to

HR Insider Tip: Key Points to Writing a Good Job Description

When writing a job description, here's a quick list of what to include:
- Job title
- The supervisor's title, not name
- Essential functions of the job
- Secondary responsibilities
- Knowledge, skills, abilities, and qualifications required for the position
- The physical and work environment.

When there's a small staff, everyone has to wear multiple hats, so you can't necessarily capture everything in a single job description. Instead, outline the basic purpose for the job and include one or two sentences about why the position exists. Don't go overboard by including nonessential functions. Simply add, "All other duties, as assigned." That covers the rest and prevents employees from being able to use the old chestnut, "That's not in my job description."

hear the responsibilities of the job from you and not from an injured employee. The employee may want extra time off work or want to return to work before they are ready (which can create the risk for additional injury).

I also highly recommend including knowledge, skills, abilities, and qualifications (KSAQs) in a job description. This is where you talk about the soft skills necessary for the job — the characteristics, traits, and education/training/experience that support an individual's ability to be successful in the job — such as excellent time-management skills or in-depth understanding of a computer programming language. These are the building blocks that employees bring with them, ready to put to use.

Want to get honest and real here? Involve your employees in developing the job descriptions for their own roles. Not only will they take more ownership of the job description process, but no one knows the job better than the employee doing it. Working with your employees to develop the job descriptions will also reveal the additional tasks they've assigned themselves. For example, your accounts manager may be the one who covers breaks for the receptionist, but if your accounts manager leaves, someone else will have to take over the task.

Involve your employees in developing the job descriptions for their own roles. Not only will they take more ownership of the job description process, but no one knows the job better than the employee doing it.

No matter what tasks your employees take on or assign to themselves, you still have the final say. You can allow them to continue or tell them to cease and desist with a certain activity, such as lifting the 50-pound jug onto the water cooler. When employees are a part of job description development, they'll have a better understanding of how they fit into and contribute to the overall success of the company.

Great Job Descriptions Reduce Drama

When a company has fantastic job descriptions, some really good things happen. First, you and your employees are crystal clear on responsibilities and the responsibilities of their coworkers and supervisors. It brings a great deal of clarity to interpersonal work relationships, defining where one job stops, where another begins, and how they are all interconnected. It gives employees boundaries; they may offer to help another coworker with their task, but they are no longer obligated or pressured to do so.

If you have an injured worker or an employee who comes to you and says they have a disability, great job descriptions (i.e., those that are accurate, thorough, and clear) put you ahead of the game. You can't be accused of creating something after the fact because you can honestly say, "We've had these descriptions in place for six months now."

Great job descriptions also make it simpler to do performance evaluations. Instead of wasting time thinking about what should be evaluated, it's all right in front of you. Job descriptions can also help you uncover redundancies and duplicated efforts between departments or roles.

Great job descriptions also make it simpler to do performance evaluations. Instead of wasting time thinking about what should be evaluated, it's all right in front of you.

One of my clients did an exercise where the company's employees had to come up with their own job descriptions. The CEO and the

COO looked over them, everybody contributed input, and they got to what they felt were the final drafts. From there, my responsibility was to take the essential functions from each individual job and put them into a big matrix. In doing that, we improved efficiency by moving some tasks out of one person's job and into another person's job, where it made more sense.

It's not unusual to discover that the fundraising/development person is covering some marketing responsibilities (even though there was a marketing/communications person on staff) or that the accountant is doing a little light HR. Look at your data, and reassign tasks to the appropriate positions so that your employees can get back to doing what they were hired to do and what they're best at doing.

When Job Descriptions Are Non-Existent

It's not unusual for small or even medium-sized businesses to have employees for whom there are no formal, written job descriptions. You may not realize that you *need* a job description until urgent circumstances or disruptions arise. Perhaps one of your employees gets hurt at work and you have to talk to their doctor, or someone is threatening to call the DOL, or there's suddenly infighting amongst your employees over who's supposed to do what ... and the drama has reached a fever pitch.

If there's a workers' compensation issue and you have to make up a job description on the spot, you can be accused of crafting it to suit your immediate needs. The doctor is then put into the position of deciding who to believe — the employee, who's been doing the job for six months, or the employer, who just created the document.

One of the hidden challenges for CEOs and business owners is that it's tough for us to have job descriptions for ourselves, because we do so many jobs inside the company. For example, I'm in business development, which requires one set of skills. I am also the HR strategist, which relies on another set of skills. There are simply so many essential functions included in being a CEO that they almost go beyond definition. Perhaps the best job description for a CEO is, "Don't let the business fail and don't let anybody get hurt. And, keep the customer happy! And grow the business, and pay the bills, and …" That covers most of the bases.

One of the hidden challenges for CEOs and business owners is that it's tough for us to have job descriptions for ourselves, because we do so many jobs inside the company.

If you've already hired everyone and you're just coming to the realization that you need to clarify the job descriptions, it's not too late. Carve a little time out of a staff meeting and say, "We're going to talk about job duties and how we affect each other." An honest-and-real discussion like that builds relevance and gets the ball rolling. People are more committed to their organization if they understand how they fit into their departments and into the overall organization. It's not just about getting the tasks done, but *how* the tasks are getting done and how they interrelate.

With a little forethought and diligence, you'll find that the work you put into defining job descriptions now will pay off time and again in the months and years to come.

A Word About Job Descriptions During a Business Disruption

When an emergency occurs, be it a localized situation or an international one, job descriptions are a tool that can assist in many decisions that will need to be made. Not only do we use the phrase "essential function," we are now acquainted with the phrase "essential worker" and "essential employer."

Well-prepared and well-maintained job descriptions can assist an organization in many areas at the time of an emergency. For example, during the COVID crisis, employers had to decide:

- Could we remain open?
- If so, who had to come into the physical operation?
- Who could perform their work remotely?
- Which tasks are essential to our survival as a business?
- Which positions perform these tasks as essential functions?
- Can we combine essential functions? If so, into which job(s)?
- Who can work "hybrid" on a combination of in-office/remote?

Having the job descriptions completed and maintained on a regular basis is one less thing to worry about during a disruption.

Chapter Three
Handbooks

Handbooks are the written document of your company's culture. They are the best piece of internal branding that you have for your company. Handbooks can help drive your culture by reinforcing your mission, vision, and values.

Handbooks also reflect your company's personal tone and attitude. Are you a more formal organization? If so, your handbook is going to be written with more formal language. Is your company a more laid-back, hip, cool place? Use more industry or brand lingo and relaxed, friendly language.

There is a school of thought out there that says, "You shouldn't have a handbook, because then you're stuck with the rules." This may be so, but your handbook is so much more than your rulebook. It should be your playbook, your guidebook: full of your expectations and goals as well as what your employees can expect of *you*.

Your handbook is so much more than your rulebook. It should be your playbook, your guidebook: full of your expectations and goals as well as what your employees can expect of *you*.

It's a way to state to your employees that you're going to provide them with a safe workplace and fair and equitable salaries, wages, or benefits. It's also a way to tell them what you expect of them: to do their jobs well, to respect their coworkers, to treat the customers like family, and to restrict personal calls to breaks and lunches.

In addition, the ideal handbook should be relevant, meaningful, and user friendly. If you hand an employee a 100-page employee handbook and tell them to read it that night and sign it, they're going to wait until you're gone, flip to the final page, and sign it. You need to keep it honest and real — something they can read and refer to when they have basic questions about policy.

_____
The ideal handbook should be relevant, meaningful, and user friendly. Honest and real!
_____

Some individual policies detailed in employee handbooks are 15-20 pages of single-spaced information — for one policy! That level of detail doesn't need to be in the handbook. Instead of including your whole drug-free workplace policy, simply state, "We are a drug-free employer and, as such, we follow an in-depth policy. For additional information and specifics on the policy, please see the drug-free workplace policy manual." In most cases, it's enough to let them know you have it (and where to find it).

To Handbook or Not to Handbook ...

It's completely up to you whether or not you have a company handbook but consider this: it's better to *not* have a handbook than to have a handbook you don't enforce. Enforcing the rules *sometimes* (or enforcing *some* policies but not others) will bite you in the end.

HR Insider Tip: How Long Is Too Long?

When it comes to handbook length, short and sweet is best. Some handbooks become more of a procedure manual than a true handbook. The two are not the same. Get your message across as succinctly as possible. If certain sections are getting long, it's probably a sign that a separate procedure manual is needed for that step.

Enforcing the rules *sometimes* (or enforcing *some* policies but not others) will bite you in the end.

Say I terminate an employee for a violation of our policy against theft from coworkers. The evidence is clear: I've seen them take food and trinkets off desks, and the whole thing is on video, so I terminate them. At the unemployment hearing, I win, but the former employee chooses to appeal. At the appeal hearing, the investigator asks, "Do you have an employee handbook? Do you have a policy against theft in the workplace? Did the employee sign the acknowledgment?" It looks like things are going great until the employee who took the food pipes up and says, "They also have an attendance policy. I've been late for work every week for a year, and I never got in trouble for that. How do I know which rules are real?" Because of your inconsistencies, the employee will likely get away with petty theft *and* get unemployment insurance benefits (i.e., checks in the mail). If you're not going to enforce something, take it out of the handbook.

I'd rather walk into an unemployment hearing and say that I don't have a theft policy, but that it's common sense that stealing is wrong. The investigator will likely agree, and chances are the employee will not be getting unemployment this time around.

Because you should enforce everything set forth in your handbook, you shouldn't offer something to employees that you aren't required to offer. One thing I see companies offering unnecessarily is family medical leave, which is governed by the Family Medical Leave Act (FMLA).

If a company has fewer than 50 employees in a 75-mile radius, it is not required that the company offer family medical leave under the FMLA. That doesn't mean the company can't offer something similar. If the company believes in and can provide 12 weeks off for an employee under circumstances similar to the FMLA requirements, then by all means, it should offer a similar policy.

Circumstances for Which Family Medical Leave May Be Required[1]

- To care for a newborn child, so long as leave is completed before the child's first birthday
- Placement of a child for adoption or foster care, so long as leave is completed before the one-year anniversary of the initial placement
- To care for a spouse, child, or parent of an employee who requires such care because of a serious health condition
- Because the employee has a serious health condition that renders them unable to perform their job

---

1 https://www.dol.gov/agencies/whd/fact-sheets/28f-fmla-qualifying-reasons

- To care for an immediate family member who is active in the Armed Forces, including a member of the National Guard or Reserves, who is undergoing medical treatment, recuperation, or therapy, is otherwise in outpatient status, or is otherwise on the temporary disability retired list for a serious injury or illness (may provide for more than 12 weeks)
- Any qualifying exigency (as the Secretary of Labor shall, by regulation, determine) arising out of the fact that the spouse, son, daughter, or parent of the employee is on active duty (or has been notified of an impending call or order to active duty) in the Armed Forces in support of a contingency operation

The challenge with offering FMLA coverage when it's not required is that as soon as you do, it's written in stone. Further, if you manage it incorrectly, you're going to be held to the same standards as a company that *is* required to offer it.

Let me say one last thing about handbooks ... If you have challenges with an employee, you can use the handbook to help guide you through an honest-and-real conversation. You could say, "You know what, Jim, I'm noticing that we are having more and more discussions about policy violations and lack of respect for your coworkers. Let's have a conversation about why that's happening."

_____
If you have challenges with an employee, you can use the handbook to help guide you through an honest-and-real conversation.
_____

In meetings with frustrated employees, walk through the handbook and revisit the expectations to see if anything throws up a red flag. Help the employees pinpoint why they're upset. They may hate wearing a suit and tie every day or may be challenged by a typical 9-to-5 schedule. Using the handbook as a tool, you can show them that a dress code and a fixed start time are there in black and white. Let them know that you're not going to change the rules and expectations. If they're not okay with that, offer some suggestions for places that might be a better fit and come up with an exit strategy.

A Word on Procedures

Your handbook is basically a policy that represents your expectations. Procedures are *behind* your expectations. For example, say that there is a company policy regarding random drug testing. This policy is outlined in the handbook, but the handbook doesn't need to contain the procedure of how participants are randomly selected, where they're going to go, how they're going to give their sample, or what's going to happen when the sample comes back. But I *have* a procedure, especially with something like drug testing, because I want to be sure that I am doing everything perfectly and consistently every time.

You can also have procedures behind your job descriptions. For example, if an employee is responsible for answering a heavy volume of calls, you might create a procedure that details how to go about answering a high volume of calls.

Procedures are much more likely to change than policies, especially when it comes to procedures that involve technological updates. It's important to note that if your procedures are woven through your handbooks, you'll have to reissue updates or the whole thing every time something changes.

In building a handbook, remember to cover the basics, include any required notices or policies (such as FMLA) keep it short, keep it simple, promote company culture, celebrate your perks, and make it something meaningful that employees will not only read but also refer to when they want to make sure they're in alignment with the rules.

A Word about Handbooks During a Business Disruption

Who would have ever thought a handbook would, literally, end up dog-eared and ragged? That's what can happen during a disruption. Even in a day-to-day situation when dealing with an employee, your handbook should be your reference manual; it should be the first place you turn when considering work hours, dealing with illnesses and leaves, and handling personal concerns, just to name a few. But during a disruption, you and your handbook may become inseparable. Frankly, before March 2020, I never considered adding a "National Emergency Preparedness" section to a handbook; now I have them in every handbook we prepare.

Before March 2020, I never considered adding a "National Emergency Preparedness" section to a handbook; now I have them in every handbook we prepare.

Today, regardless of the size of the company, having some type of documentation, whether it be in a handbook or in a binder on a shelf, can be priceless. Business leaders are people too (we often forget that) and we get nervous and anxious just like our employees. In fact, we not only worry about ourselves, but we worry about our employees and their families as well. Having a prepared policy or document that we can turn to that has been prepared in advance of a disruption can only 1) help us move forward and 2) assuage some of the jitters.

Chapter Four
Record Keeping

You will constantly hear me singing the praises of good record keeping. It's the best way to protect yourself, to prepare for employee meetings and evaluations, and to be at the ready should an agency or lawyer ever knock on your door.

In the "good ol' days" of personnel departments, everything went into one personnel file. Files would be inches thick, and we never got rid of anything — who knew when you might need to know what deductions Johnny had authorized in 1964? (If we did get rid of anything, it went right in the trash can; there were no shredders in those days — less identity theft way back then, too.)

Later, the Immigration Reform and Control Act of 1986 was enacted to reduce the employment of undocumented immigrants. The I-9 Form provided a list of various types of acceptable documents — specifically, documentation that may indicate an employee's national origin and race (protected classes). To the best of my recollection, that was when we began separating personnel documents into different files. Next, came the Americans with Disabilities Act of 1990 (ADA), which required employers to keep medical records confidential, and the Health Insurance Portability and Accountability Act of 1996 (HIPAA.) With HIPAA came the new phrase *protected health information* ("PHI"), reinforcing creation of a second file for medical records. I, affectionately, call this the "super-secret red file!"

With HIPAA came the new phrase *protected health information* ("PHI"), reinforcing creation of a second file for medical records. I, affectionately, call this the "super-secret red file!"

This file was to include any and all information about an employee's medical and health information, including benefit enrollment forms (and information about their dependents).

A few important things to remember:

- You have a duty to protect your employees' personal information, paying particular attention to Social Security numbers, dates of birth, and personal health information.
- Access to employee files* should be on a need-to-know basis.
- Files should be kept secure with limited accessibility; medical files should be maintained in a confidential, separate file area with even less accessibility.
- I-9s should be kept separate from personnel and medical files, but they may be kept in a single, company-wide file — we prefer a 3-ring binder.
- Old information should be shredded, not simply thrown away, especially if it contains any information that could identify an employee.

When in doubt, err on the side of caution. Ask yourself if you would want the particular document or piece of information revealed about you personally, and treat it with that same respect.

*While it's fair to say that the concept of "personnel" is gone forever, there's some curiosity in the fact that HR professionals still call employee files "personnel files." When it comes to record-keeping, old habits about terminology, it seems, die hard.

Sample Personnel File Checklist

The "Traditional" File

- ☐ Employment application, resume and offer letter
- ☐ Reference checks
- ☐ College transcripts
- ☐ Job descriptions
- ☐ Records relating to the job: hiring, promotion, demotion, transfer, layoff, rates of pay, as well as other forms of compensation, and education and training records
- ☐ Records relating to employment practices
- ☐ Letters of recognition
- ☐ Disciplinary notices or documents
- ☐ Performance evaluations
- ☐ Test documents used in an employment decision
- ☐ Exit interviews
- ☐ Termination records

The "Medical" File

- ☐ Medical/insurance records
- ☐ Physical/drug screen results
- ☐ Doctors' notes
- ☐ FMLA certification and/or ADA documents
- ☐ Requests for employment/payroll verification
- ☐ Child support/garnishments
- ☐ Vaccination Cards

The "Someplace Else" File

- ☐ I-9 form
- ☐ Safety training records
- ☐ Litigation documents
- ☐ Worker's Compensation Claims

> **When in doubt, err on the side of caution. Ask yourself if you would want the particular document or piece of information revealed about you personally, and treat it with that same respect.**

If you have commercial motor vehicle operators at your company, you need a driver qualification ("DQ") file. This should have copies of all appropriate certifications and licenses for driving commercial motor vehicles, background checks, annual State Motor Vehicle Reports (MVRs), and the driver medical certification card. You should keep the DQ file separate from your other files (but equally confidential).

It's not uncommon to need additional records, such as training certifications, child abuse clearances, drug testing, clearance documents, and fingerprinting. Just make sure that you know whether each document regards general employment or is protected. If it's protected, it should be in the confidential file.

Human resources is a paperwork-intensive business function. Many companies, however, are converting (or have completely converted) to electronic files. If that is the case for your company, make sure that those electronic files are as secure as a locked safe, with protections, access codes, and safety assurances. To be honest, with all the hacking that takes place in today's world, a good old, locked filing cabinet often provides the most secure — and affordable — protection.

> **With all the hacking that takes place in today's world, a good old, locked filing cabinet often provides the most secure protection.**

The benefit to keeping files on hand in paper form is that they are easy to access and share when an agency comes calling. With electronic files, you can always print out what's needed, but you need to remember that once confidential files are out of the computer, they must still be protected properly.

Ensuring your employees' right to privacy is your responsibility, and it's a responsibility you should take seriously.

A Word About Record-Keeping During a Business Disruption

COVID created a whole new record-keeping (nightmare) scenario. Daily temperature checks, symptom-free affidavits, test results, vaccination cards. Companies were also to retain applications/support for Family First Coronavirus Response Act (FFCRA) pay because they would be receiving tax credits for any payments issued to employees.

At the end of the day, employee confidentiality still needs to be upheld, regardless of any disruptions. HIPAA is still in place, rightfully so, even when we have supervisors doing temperature checks. Be prepared and be sure your supervisors understand their responsibilities.

Part Two

Bringing People on Board

Chapter Five
Recruiting

Finding the right person for the job is critical, not just because you need to fill a position but because bringing in someone new can affect your office culture (and office culture affects how much drama comes knocking on your door). But if you do things right, you can end up with a great new hire who helps your company be successful for years to come. Do things wrong and, well …

People often look at recruiting as *selection*. I prefer to see recruiting as *sourcing to find the right person*. Instead of focusing on finding a miracle candidate, you want to focus on the very real possibility of finding lots of good candidates to consider.

> **I prefer to see recruiting as *sourcing to find the right person*.**

Unlike job descriptions, where the main focus is to know what you're looking for, recruiting is all about finding a pool of candidates who can do what you need them to do. To accomplish this, you need to know the hard skills (for the actual tasks) that the person will require, and you need to consider the soft skills (the characteristics or traits) that will ensure their success in the job *and* in your organization.

Using our example of a receptionist, the hard skill needed might be "able to answer phone calls," but there's more to it than that. Do you want someone who can answer the phone pleasantly and have a conversation with the caller? Or do you prefer someone who's a bit more direct? If you have a lot of incoming calls, you'll want the receptionist to find out where each call needs to go and move the calls along quickly. That takes certain soft skills, like being direct and focused on efficiency. Chattier individuals would be terribly uncomfortable in an environment where they need to move calls through like cows in a cattle chute. Their soft skills might be an ability to make everyone feel like an old friend or to calm nerves. Both have value; it just depends on what your company needs.

Soft skills are just as important as hard skills — maybe more so. We can train hard skills — typing, tightening bolts on a piece of machinery, transferring data — but it's much more difficult to train someone to answer the phone pleasantly.

_____

We can train hard skills — typing, tightening bolts on a piece of machinery, transferring data — but it's much more difficult to train someone to answer the phone pleasantly.
_____

Each position actually has two different sets of soft skills: company soft skills (characteristics that everyone in the organization must be able to demonstrate) and job-specific soft skills, which apply to that particular position only. Everyone at HR Resolutions (my company) needs to embrace and get that "HR is Fun!" (company soft skills). Our HR coordinator also needs to be very detail-oriented, while our project manager needs to have broad thinking skills with the ability to see the big picture (job-specific soft skills).

When recruiting, many CEOs feel like they know the positions they're hiring for, inside and out. But let's go back to why we *document, document, document*. I want you to be able to protect yourself in three weeks from the person that you *didn't* hire. If there's an issue or accusation, you want to be able to refer to your documentation and say, "This is what we were looking for before we even met you or started looking to fill the position. Based on our interview, you did not demonstrate the traits or characteristics needed to be successful in the position. For example ..."

Like a playbook helps a team win a football game, determining what you need now and putting it down on paper will help you write your recruitment ad, determine the questions you're going to ask during screenings and interviews, evaluate how the candidates have done in the interviews, and, ultimately, make your selection. You're setting yourself up for success and making the hiring process easier.

Setting things down in stone also helps prevent you from hiring people for jobs they're not suited for just because you really like their personalities. (If someone came in who also adopted retired racing greyhounds, I'd naturally think they were perfect for whatever job needed doing!) It's human nature to identify with someone when you have a connection, but loving retired greyhounds isn't going to get the payroll done accurately or on time.

Time, Budget, and Location

If you want to optimize your recruiting process, there are three things to think about: time, budget, and location.

As you plan your recruiting strategy, you need to consider how quickly you need to find someone. The shorter timeframe you have in which to find someone, the wider you should cast your net from the beginning. Did your operations manager give you a one-month notice? Is this a newly created position? Do you have a little time to shop around, or is this a critical position to fill as quickly as possible? If the search is for your vice president of operations and you don't get someone in that position pronto, then you're going to have to do *that* job along with *your own* job, which adds a bit more urgency to the situation.

To keep yourself from overspending during the search, you need a recruiting budget. Know how much money you have and how you want to spend it. Just remember — you get what you pay for! I've had some great successes with Craigslist.org, but that tends to run hot and cold because the right person has to be looking on the right day. A website like Indeed.com, which has both free and paid options, draws a more work-focused crowd. The big paid online sites, such as Monster.com and CareerBuilder.com, draw from all over the world and have advanced algorithms working behind the scenes. The services and programs change almost daily.

When it comes to a recruiting budget, just remember — you get what you pay for!

As you scout locations to place your job ads, keep in mind that you are looking to find the passive job-seeker — the individual who's basically happy in their current job but is curious about what else is out there. Those people tend to go to the bigger, better-known sites, because they assume that way is quicker and faster (and it often is); but in some towns, it's still the local paper that gets all the hits.

Let's look more deeply into the importance of choosing where to advertise. If you're hiring for a warehouse person, you don't need to be doing a national search. The likelihood of someone moving across the country for a warehouse job is fairly low. But if you're looking for the dean of a college, a national search makes sense.

Where you advertise depends upon the position (and position level) in question. Bring in as many options as possible! The more specific the job and the higher up the ladder you go, the wider you'll have to cast your net. Lots of people can work as a cashier; fewer can blow a perfect piece of glass for a museum-quality vase or manage a national sales team in three languages.

> **The Newspaper:** You can spend more on a newspaper ad than you could for a 30-day or 60-day job posting on paid websites, but in certain towns and for certain types of jobs, people still use the newspaper as their go-to source.
>
> **Trade Associations:** If you're a book or magazine publisher, utilize your publishing associations. If you're a trucking company, utilize the American Trucking Association. Trade/industry associations are a fantastic resource and are usually a cost-effective way to advertise to precisely the people you're looking for.
>
> **Industry Job Boards:** Most industries have trade sites that include job boards. For example, in the theater industry, there are websites like Playbill.com that cater to people who are passionate about theater and that list jobs related to the industry. The same goes for nonprofits dealing with the arts, health, animal welfare, or any number of other categories. If you're looking for an office manager, why not find one who also happens to be passionate about your industry or cause?
>
> **Chamber of Commerce:** The Chamber of Commerce works to connect businesspeople and is focused on business success and

growth. The Rotary Club or other business associations also fall into this category.

Unemployment Office: This is the source that nearly everyone forgets about, and they shouldn't. The unemployment office is a fantastic resource that is often underutilized because people tend to think of it as a place that draws from the bottom of the barrel. That is completely untrue. Outside of starting my own company, the best job I ever got came through my local unemployment office. Better still, recruiting through the unemployment office is free! You should post every single job opening you ever have with them.

_____

Outside of starting my own company, the best job I ever got came through my local unemployment office.

_____

When considering location, you should also think about populations of people that you may be overlooking. Thinking outside the standard corporate box can lead you to some truly exceptional candidates.

Veterans: Don't forget your military Veterans. They have had incredible training and know how to work as part of a team. In my area, we have Fort Indiantown Gap, which is associated with the Pennsylvania National Guard, but nearly every town in America has a Veterans' organization or a VA office. There's a national trend to establish organizations as "Veteran-ready businesses," with win-win opportunities — to attract top talent from among men and women making the transition from active duty to civilian careers, and to do so while building your company's brand as supportive of those who have served in the Armed Forces.

Seniors: AARP isn't necessarily a euphemism for *old people*. You can join AARP when you're 50 or older. Older employees offer a wealth of experience and understanding that can be a welcome resource in any business. For most senior and executive positions, AARP (which has a top-notch magazine and a huge social media following) can be a smart place to connect with job prospects.

People with Disabilities or Physical Challenges: You absolutely should not discount this population in your area. *Disabled* does not mean crippled or unable to work. It means that someone is working with a physical challenge and may need accommodations. I think that sometimes people overlook this part of the population because they're not sure how to incorporate an individual with physical challenges into their work environment. According to the Centers for Disease Control and Prevention, approximately 60% of adults have a chronic disease.[1] And there's a simple solution to addressing your knowledge gaps about how to fully accommodate employees with different abilities or needs. Just contact any of your local nonprofit agencies that deal with individuals with disabilities and challenges. A quick internet search of "office of vocational rehab" or "disability services" should provide you with a great deal of resources that will gladly help you determine which positions might be a good match. The Job Accommodation Network (JAN) is also a great resource: www.askjan.org.

People in Transition and People Returning to the Workforce: As a country, I think Americans are still of a mindset that when you make a job change, you should make more money. That's not the case anymore. Don't discount someone just because they're stepping out of management and want to go back into customer service. First, they know enough of what they want that they've

---

[1] https://www.cdc.gov/chronicdisease/resources/infographic/chronic-diseases.htm

left a good position to start over. Second, there is value in having people who are knowledgeable about several positions and fields. Similarly, don't discount someone who is returning to the workforce after taking time away. Many talented people in our workforce are often those who have chosen to take a career break for any number of reasons; career re-launchers are a treasure trove of skills and character. Don't miss out on talent because there is a gap in a resume.

It's important to remember that people who look the shiniest on the resume page aren't always the clearest when they step into the interview. Go back to the essential functions of the position. Who is best qualified to do the job? Let the essential functions lead you to the right person.

It's important to remember that people who look the shiniest on the resume page aren't always the clearest when they step into the interview. Let the essential functions of thr position lead you to the right person.

Writing the Recruitment Ad

Let's start with brass tacks: Never put the entire job description into the ad. I don't care how much room you have — an ad is not a job description; it's an opportunity to advertise and sell your company.

Use the recruitment ad to talk about the great things that your company offers and what it can do for an individual. Attract potential candidates so they say, "I want to find out more!" Then, put in your minimum qualifications — a combination of hard and soft

HR Insider Tip: Applicant Tracking Systems (ATS)

These software system solutions enable you to do several things, and depending upon your volume of recruiting, you should seriously consider your options.

1. Write the ad once.

2. The ATS posts the job on MULTIPLE boards (for example, the system we use sends the job to 18 free sites).

3. ALL responses come to one spot (and NOT your email inbox).

4. You can establish "knock-out" questions that will automatically qualify or disqualify an applicant.

5. You can track everything that happens with each applicant, so your recordkeeping is already built into the system (see "tracking responses" below).

skills. Don't put too much in, or you might scare people off if they don't match bullet point #19 in your lengthy ad.

You should also use your recruitment ad as your first line of screening. If a bachelor's degree is needed to be successful in the position, that should be in the ad.

This was a real ad on Craigslist ... **THIS IS BAD.**

> **CDL Driver Qualification File Specialist**
>
> I need someone experienced with creating and maintaining CDL Driver Qualification files. (DQ files)
>
> We hire hundreds of CDL drivers per year, so you must be independent and knowledgable. [sic]
>
> Please email your resume and salary requirements.

Here is a better version.

> **CDL Driver Qualification File Specialist**
>
> Seeking a team member who can work independently and is up-to-date on DQ requirements. Opportunity to create and develop our systems to stay compliant in a constantly changing environment. Please respond with your current resume and salary requirements. We are an Equal Opportunity Employer.

Note the Differences:

- "Knowledgeable" vs. "Knowledgable" — FYI ... spelling counts in ads.
- Use the lingo — if they have experience, they'll know the lingo.
- Be positive.

- Don't assume they are going to send a current resume — require it.

Tracking Responses

I like to track everything. I want to know who has responded from what source, so that I can evaluate whether or not a source is working for me. I want to see my return on investment, even from a free ad. Am I getting qualified candidates from my Craigslist ads? (Because if I'm getting sufficient candidates from a free ad, to heck with the paid ads the next time!) If you don't track it, you'll never know.

You can track and screen on a very simple Excel spreadsheet where you list the individuals' names and how they heard about the job opening. You might list minimum requirements across the top and then build in columns for hard skills, soft skills, salary history, and anecdotal notes.

As responses come in, record everything — who they are, what ad location they come from, and if they meet the minimum qualifications. The more boxes a candidate checks, the higher the likelihood that you should invite them in for an interview. In a situation where you are accused of discriminating during hiring, you can present that document and say, "This individual was not considered because we hired based on these factors, and they did not do as well as such and such other candidate. It had nothing to do with their age, color, national origin, sex, religion, or any other protected classification."

As you proceed, you can add to that tracked data with the date of the interview and your interview ranking. That way, it's all right there in a single document. You can make a chart in your notebook, in Excel, or as a Word file. The key is simply to track all your interviews in one place; it doesn't matter how you do it.

Creating an interview ranking is much like screening your responses. You should actually conduct your interview and evaluate that interview *immediately* after you've done it, before you see anyone else. You want to make sure that the candidate meets the expectations and that you're interviewing for the things you're actually seeking. Don't let debrief conversations with colleagues or others impact your evaluation. Rank the interview with the experience is fresh in your mind.

These objective measurements using a clear evaluation process, perhaps with a rubric where you used points to measure qualifications and fit, can help reinforce in your mind why you should select one candidate and not another. It helps you on two levels — one, in choosing the best person for the job and not the one who you are most drawn to on a personal level; and two, to streamline the

HR Insider Tip: Typos on Resumes

There's a key reason for tossing resumes that are full of mistakes: If I run an ad and I get 300 responses for one customer service position, I need to reduce that number of responses for review. Or, if the ability to write accurate, eloquent, grammatically correct documents is one of the soft skills I'm seeking, the resume already gives me an idea of whether the candidate is qualified. You don't need to be a perfect speller to be an excellent candidate for other positions though, so think about what you're looking for before you toss a resume in the trash. You should be keeping the resumes for a couple months anyway, in case there ever is an issue.

process and gather valuable data, should you ever need to defend your decisions.

A final note on recruiting: Culture building should really start from the recruiting ad! Let people know what's important to you even before the interview — that way, there's an increased chance that you'll attract people who share the organization's values and cultural vibe. Being up front about your culture ensures a good match when it comes to candidates.

The thing to remember in all of this is that by spending a little time now, you are saving yourself huge amounts of time later, all while driving yourself toward the best candidate available.

A Word About Recruiting During Business Disruption

The onset of the COVID-19 crisis was a confusing time for all employers — whether you were deemed "essential" or not. Heading into the pandemic (i.e., in 2019), I often talked about how it was the worst recruiting market I had ever experienced. Please take this as a lesson to be careful what you say — it's 100 times worse now for any number of reasons.

Disruptions, such as a pandemic (or a war or a flood or fire), really drive employers to determine exactly the staff that are necessary to keep the business moving. This has a huge impact upon recruiting — do I move internal staff into openings to protect their employment? Do I go outside while I'm still displacing internal staff? Do I really need to fill this position right now? If so, what will the position look like when this is over?

All these questions need to be resolved before moving forward. If you DO decide to move forward to external recruiting, a *critical* spot to use for recruiting is your local unemployment commission's on-line job board, especially during times of massive, cross-industry job reductions. Honestly, people do want to work.

Chapter Six
Interviewing

So, you've thrown out your net, recruited, found as many candidates as possible for consideration, evaluated their initial responses, screened them, and determined if they should move to the next level. Interviewing is where the rubber meets the road. But now, instead of trying to draw people in, the purpose shifts to screening people out. Your job now is to find the ideal candidate.

The biggest mistake that interviewers make is that they talk too much. An interviewer should only talk about 20 percent of the time. This is the candidate's opportunity to shine. I think the reason that interviewers talk too much is that they're nervous, and the cure for those nerves is to be prepared. Know what you're doing before you walk into that room. Know what you're going to say, what questions you're going to ask, and what will fulfill your requirements.

The biggest mistake that interviewers make is that they talk too much.

Another common mistake I see is when people try to make friends with candidates, instead of truly interviewing them. Everyone wants to be liked, but that should not be the focus of your interview. Be professional and pleasant, but don't try to be the candidate's buddy. There are a number of interview styles that can be employed to reveal different characteristics and skills. It's critical to know what you want to learn *before* you go into the interview process, so you can prepare any necessary questions to help you discover those things, both good and bad. Keep in mind, these could be characteristics/qualifications you are seeking or ones you wish to avoid.

A **one-on-one interview** is the traditional method where the candidate meets alone with the interviewer. Questions are asked, hopefully by both parties, to determine if it's a good fit and whether the candidate fulfills the hard and soft requirements of the position.

Group interviews are helpful in certain circumstances where you might want to see how someone functions as part of a team or in a group environment. Or you may need to find multiple candidates for a single job description, like a position in retail sales or food service. Group interviews are also an effective tool at finding upper-level candidates, as this interview style often reveals who demonstrates natural leadership and/or diplomacy skills.

A **stress interview** is a high-pressure situation that reveals how a candidate may react in a tense environment. I highly recommend these for salespeople, as a test of skill and effectiveness under pressure. In a stress interview, you keep drilling down on one thing, searching for a breaking point *or* asking questions in a rapid-fire approach in order to see how the candidate will react

Rote interviews are very "yes and no." You ask a series of questions, looking for specific answers such as the following:

"*Can you type?*"

"*Yes.*"

"Can you work 8:00 a.m. to 5:00 p.m.?"

"Yes."

"Can you make a chart in Excel?"

"I don't know, but I'm good with computers."

"Have you answered phones before?"

"Yes."

"Can you start Monday?"

"Yes."

"Great, you've got the job, and we'll train you in Excel."

A ***behavioral interview*** is the exact opposite of the rote method. Instead of asking yes or no questions, ask questions that require the candidate to talk, describe, and explain. It's basically a conversation designed to discover if candidates have the hard and soft skills you need.

A ***motivation-based interview*** goes even further and tells us so much more about the candidate's *specific* skill experience, locus of control (internal or external), and career match. Locus of control is a psychological term that helps us determine if a person believes *they* control their world (internal) or if *other* forces control their world (external). For example, someone whose approach hinges on "well, policy says …" would be someone with an external locus — the "policy" dictates the outcome. An internal locus would drive someone else to say, "policy says this, but let's see what I can do to dictate the outcome." My experience has shown me that we're hiring better quality candidates using this methodology. I generally start out all my interviews — which tend to be heavily "motivation-based" in nature, with, "I'm going to ask you a few questions because I want to better understand your background." And that's exactly what an interview should be: an attempt to better understand the candidate's background and fit.

> **HR Insider Tip: Interviewing**
>
> For more on Motivation-Based Interviewing (MBI), check out *the* interview-training expert — Carol Quinn — at hireauthority.com. MBI is the first thing in my profession to make me go *Hmmm* in a long time!

If I need a detail-oriented person, I might ask, "Tell me about a specific time you were given limited instruction for a new project." If I have an individual that answers by walking me through the project details on a chronological path, that is a sign to me that this candidate is a detail-oriented person. A creative thinker will likely answer by describing their favorite task first and working down and around the project tasks. The motivation-based interview has revealed this candidate may not be the kind of detail-oriented person I'm looking for, but that they might be the perfect person to place in a creative role that's supported by a project manager who will be juggling all the details while the creative leader focuses on creation and innovation.

As always, select your questions ahead of time, and ask each candidate the same questions. In a motivation-based interview, your focus is on listening. You don't have time to think of what you'll say next. Let the questions guide you and consider if you must probe a little deeper into candidates' answers.

In all forms of interviewing, having your questions in place beforehand is not only a great organizational strategy, but a protective one. If all candidates are asked the same questions, it will be harder to pursue any kind of discrimination claim about why someone did or did not get the job. You also want to be sure to determine what answers meet your expectations and will support success in the position — developing a rating form or rubric with more details of positive/negative examples is even better.

Be sure to select your questions ahead of time, and ask each candidate the same questions. In all forms of interviewing, having your questions in place beforehand is not only a great organizational strategy, but a protective one.

The Interview Process

All interviews, no matter what style, should follow this same simple pattern: the opening, the actual interview, the closing, and the evaluation.

When you first sit down to interview someone, you want to put them at ease. If you're feeling nervous about interviewing, you may choose to break the ice by saying, "For what it's worth, I find interviews a little nerve-wracking myself, no matter which side of the desk I'm sitting on. But it's exciting to meet someone new and see how their talents might fit our company, so I like to focus on being excited instead of nervous. Does that make sense?" Being real and revealing something about yourself, or relating to the charged emotion, will place the interviewee at ease, as does providing insight into your interview process.

Let the candidate know you're going to have a conversation: you want to understand their background a little bit better, you'll talk about the position, and they will have an opportunity to ask you questions before talking about next steps. This describes the complete process in full clarity.

Proceed through your interview, as planned, with your questions at the ready.

In closing an interview, make sure all your questions have been answered. Then ask, "What questions do you have for me?" Candidates might ask me what I like about the company and why I choose to work here. They might ask why the position is open. I don't care what they ask, as long as they ask me *something*. Asking a question demonstrates their interest in the job and shows that they were paying attention during the interview. And here is the perfect spot to be honest and real: answer their questions truthfully, even if you think the answer doesn't place the company in the best light. That's their decision — not yours. Don't sugarcoat or cover up drama at work! That just leads to more drama down the road.

When the interview is over, I'll say, "Thank you for coming in. We have several interviews scheduled, but we anticipate making a decision and moving on to the next step by this time next week." I let them know what the next steps are, and then stand, shake their hand, and gesture toward the door or walk them out.

It's critical to evaluate the interview before moving on to the next candidate. Fill out your rating form and mark your boxes. For example, you may have been looking for three soft skills: dependability, customer service, and detail orientation. Write the numbers directly into your form. Do this before you pick up your smartphone, before you look at your e-mail, and before you answer your voicemail.

It's critical to evaluate the interview before moving on to the next candidate.

Do not skip this step! The interview isn't really over until the candidate has left and you have finished recording your evaluation into your chart. Even if you're a trained, skilled interviewer, if you have three interviews in one day and wait until the end of the day to evaluate them, you are not going to remember with total clarity who said what. Evaluate the candidate and set the paper aside, until you are completely finished with the interviewing process.

A Note About Phone Screening

If a candidate's resume and cover letter initially meet three out of four of your desired criteria, you may move that person to the next step in the process, which is a phone screening. Phone screenings help you fill in details and get additional information before deciding whether or not to continue to the next level of the hiring process.

Talking to a candidate on the phone can take up a lot less time than a face-to-face interview and requires less commitment on the parts of both the employer and the potential employee. It's a good way for both of you to decide if you'd like to move forward.

During the screening, you should have three or four questions that will help you gain more information about the candidate. Again, you'll evaluate how they did on those questions based upon the essential functions and requirements of the position before determining if the candidate will move on to the next step: interviewing.

When Drama Happens

There are a lot of things that can go wrong during an interview that are difficult to defend later. Perhaps you don't have any notes from the interview. Perhaps you do have notes, but they show that you asked every candidate a different set of questions or spent hugely varied amounts of time with people.

For example, maybe you only spent a few minutes with one candidate, and you ended up hiring him because he was Uncle James's second cousin. But you spent a full 10 minutes with the minority candidate (who you *didn't* actually consider) and, for seven of those minutes, all you did was talk. You didn't ask any questions. You didn't allow that candidate the opportunity to demonstrate that they were qualified for the position.

With the correct process in place, however, you're protected. It gives you a way to let down Uncle James's second cousin because you can say, "We treated you the same way we did everybody else. The person we hired demonstrated more specific experience with the skills we need for this position. We'll try to find you something in the organization." This also gives you an out with Uncle James because you have quantifiable evidence as to why you hired someone other than his second cousin. You can further explain that you cannot hire based on nepotism (or cronyism, or any "-ism"), and that his cousin wasn't going to be successful in that position anyway.

Most of all, having a correct process protects you from *you*. We are our own worst enemies: we talk too much in interviews. We collect people who are more like us than they are actually qualified. But this is all human nature, and as long as we realize where these fallacies and errors are in our selections, we can correct them.

Sample Interview Rating Form

Candidate: _____

Client: _____

Position: _____

Date: _____

Competency	Below Expectations	Meets Expectations	Exceeds Expectations
HR / Admin			
Organizational / Time Management			
Verbal Communication			
Problem Solving			
Other			

Comments: _____

_____

_____

_____

Next Steps: _____

_____

When we take time to prepare for our interviews and use the same job-related questions and format with every applicant, we reveal similarities and differences in candidate responses that are easier to compare and contrast. Instead of responding emotionally, we can make an honest, real, thoughtful, balanced decision about who is truly best for the job, often surprising ourselves with our final choice.

A Word About Interviewing During a Business Disruption

Again, I truly wish I had bought stock in Zoom or Citrix (GoToMeeting) prior to March 2020. The way in which two-way online video technologies changed our world — especially the world of HR — is almost impossible to quantify but baffling to behold. Video interviews were a life saver for interviewers and job seekers alike. The recruiting and interviewing train could not stop for open positions, yet very few people were comfortable with face-to-face meetings (nor were they recommended) during the height of the COVID-19 outbreak. Enter — the Video Interview!

Whether you are interviewing candidates face-to-face in real life or from a distance via webcams, you still have the same regulations, guidelines, and processes to follow. The only thing that has changed here is the medium for which we are interviewing. Remember, whatever you see (or think you see) in the background of their life should not come into play during the interview. Focus only on their ability to do the job regardless of the maid cleaning in the background or the greyhounds vying for their attention during the call.

Chapter Seven
Selection

Selecting the right candidate is an agonizing process, right? It's impossible to know from the interview how someone will actually behave in their job, right? *Wrong.*

When you're finished interviewing all potential candidates, pull out the evaluation sheets that you set aside and sort them from highest to lowest scores. Look at the person on the top of the stack. That's the candidate you hire.

If you followed best practices, kept your documentation and tracking going all along, and have your evaluation forms, then the process should have made your selection for you. Let the process work for you and trust it. You may be led to a surprisingly good match.

Let the process work for you and trust it. You may be led to a surprisingly good match.

Now, that doesn't mean you shouldn't do your due diligence before giving the top candidate a formal offer. Checking references is an important step in determining your final candidate, and this should be done before the offer is made. Best practice would suggest you check references on your top candidate first, as it can be somewhat time consuming.

Always ask for professional references (not personal references) and recognize that candidates are going to give you names of people who will speak favorably of them. Nine out of 10 times, the person giving the reference is going to give you the candidate's proverbial name, rank, and serial number only (i.e., will tell you very little, simply confirming the candidate's title and role at the time they worked together, maybe dates of employment, and a few other objective details). Everyone is a little afraid to provide references because they don't want to be sued for saying the wrong thing. But, if you listen closely to tone and to what information is provided, you can get much of the information you need.

HR Insider Tip: Prior Employer

Instead of asking candidates for permission to speak to a specific person, ask for permission to speak with their *prior employer*. Once you get that permission, you're cleared to talk to anyone from their immediate supervisor to their old CEO. Instead of talking to the specific reference candidates provide, you might try to find their direct manager and contact that individual. NEVER call ANYONE from the current employer unless you have CLEAR permission.

Making the Offer

Once you make your selection, you can make the offer — but don't jump the gun and reject your other candidates yet. Wait until your offer has been accepted before you let everyone else down. It's awfully embarrassing to have to go back to the number-two candidate and say, "Um, well, I know I called you yesterday and said we selected someone else, but, um, never mind! I really want you to come work for me today."

I always recommend an offer be a direct phone call to the candidate by the hiring manager. That way, the manager starts developing a relationship with their new employee right away. If that's not an option, then use your best judgment in selecting who extends the offer.

After the verbal offer has been made, be sure to follow up with an official written letter to ensure clarity. You want to make sure that everything's perfectly understood. "Here is your at-will employment offer, here is your job title, here is what your pay rate is going to be, here is your starting date, and here is where you report." In doing this, you're setting safe boundaries and further developing those new relationships. Be sure the offer is "contingent upon successfully completing" any other necessary requirements, such as a background check or drug testing.

Be cautious when asking the new employee to sign the offer letter and return it. Be sure you haven't created a contract. Be clear in your intent with the offer letter — it serves as written confirmation of your verbal offer of employment. Do *not* make it a contract. By asking for an acceptance signature, you could mistakenly be doing just that! For example, quoting an annual salary instead of a "per pay period" salary *could* give the person the understanding they will receive that full amount whether they work the full year or not. An offer letter should include at-will employment and be a confirmation of what you discussed in terms of responsibilities and compensation/benefits.

The offer letter is also another opportunity for branding: you're bringing the person into the fold to be part of the institutional family, should they accept. Having your letter reiterate what your organization stands for, whether it's a "Best Places to Work," etc., positions you better for the candidate accepting the offer, especially if they have other offers to consider.

If you have other requirements that must be met before the first day, the offer should actually be "contingent upon successful completion of our pre-employment requirements." At that point, you could run a background check and/or perform any other pre-employment, post-offer tests to confirm that you can, in good faith, employ that person without putting your other employees or clients in jeopardy.

You should not run a background check for everyone except those for whom you have extended a valid offer of employment. For one thing, there's a cost involved. The background check that you run must be tied to the job that the subject will be doing. There needs to be a *bona fide occupational job qualification* (BFOQ) attached.

For example, there's no reason to run a credit check on a receptionist, a machinist, or someone in accounts payable. Their credit has no bearing on their ability to do their jobs. However, if you're hiring a bank teller, that person is handling your money and your customers' money. While a history of credit issues won't tell you if candidates will steal or not, bad credit does indicate a higher risk that they might be tempted to help themselves to a couple dollars here or there.

If the credit check reveals poor credit, it's your duty to research *why*. Poor credit may not discount a candidate from the job (it might even be part of the reason why they need it), but do look into it and have an honest-and-real conversation with the candidate, without passing judgment. Losing your job and defaulting on your student loans is different from maxing out three new credit cards for a trip to Tahiti. I wouldn't worry if a candidate fell behind on medical bills after a one-time event. I would, however, raise an eyebrow if someone had 15 credit cards, all of which are currently over the limit. Remember that the Fair Credit Reporting Act and other federal, state, and local laws may be applicable to how you handle background checks.

HR Insider Tip: "Ban the Box" Regulations

"Ban the Box" regulations cover that one little area on job applications where you ask, "Have you ever been convicted of a crime?"

In some states and municipalities, "Ban the Box" regulations require employers to remove criminal record related questions from job applications. Does this mean that I can't check someone's criminal record in the future? It does not. If there's a BFOQ (Bona Fide Occupational Qualification) for me to check a reference, I can and will check the person's background when the time is *appropriate*. But, do I need to know if candidates have been convicted of a crime *before* I interview them? In all honesty, no. Until they're my employees — or are about to be — that's their personal business.

Background checks have been considered a consumer report for some time now, which means that they fall under the Fair Credit Reporting Act.[1] If you are doing a background check of any kind, you must provide the individual with a copy of their rights under the Fair Credit Reporting Act. This is because there are required steps you must take if you are going to pursue a negative or adverse action against an individual due to information received from a background check (such as not hiring that individual).

When looking at a criminal record report, look only at pertinent information from the past seven years. Unfortunately, some criminal reports show everything — it's hard to not look, but I strongly recommend you ignore it if it's not relevant to the job!

If I see a felony theft charge against someone who I'm hiring for a retail operation, then the offer will probably be rescinded, as that has a direct bearing on the job (a BFOQ of responsibility for retail inventory). However, if the individual has a misdemeanor charge for damage of personal goods, I'm going to have a conversation with them in order to better understand the whole story.

I once interviewed a young woman who was an ideal candidate for a position, but her background check revealed some charges that were a little questionable for a retail environment. When I had a conversation with her, she told me what happened. In high school, her friends dared her to steal a stick of lip gloss. She took the dare and was caught. Because she was over 18, it went on her record. Embarrassed, she told me she'd learned her lesson and that she now understands actions (and their consequences) can follow you forever. After that conversation, there was no reason not to bring her on board. She's now an awesome employee! But if I had not had that

---

1 A joint publication of the FTC and the Equal Employment Opportunity Commission: "Background Checks: What Employers Need to Know." https://www.eeoc.gov/laws/guidance/background-checks-what-employers-need-know

honest conversation with her, I likely would have skipped over her and moved on to someone else.

You may ask yourself, "Why do a background check at all?" The main reason is to protect yourself from something called *negligent hiring*. Imagine that I'm hiring a service technician to go into people's homes. I fail to do a background check and unwittingly hire someone convicted for armed robbery. He goes into my customer's house, cases the house during the install, and then returns later that night and robs them blind. That family can now sue me, the employer, for negligent hiring — and they should. I didn't do my due diligence and failed to protect my customers.

Rejections

Be careful how you reject someone. That person might be a future customer or a future hire, and if you don't reject them professionally, you could lose that potential individual for the long term. Plus, social media — need I say more?

Imagine that your number-two candidate for a sales job would be ideal in customer service, and next week, you have a customer service position open. You can simply skip a second hiring process and call that person to see if they are still seeking employment. But if the rejection for the other position was handled poorly, that person may say, "Um … no thanks. I don't want to work for you."

Treat everyone you interview as a potential future candidate or customer. Even if they're not right for the job, they may still be good for your business.

A Word about Selection During a Business Disruption

Recruiting is difficult — no one will argue with that. Hiring managers may be hurting for additional staff for any number of reasons and when someone is found who might be able to do the job, it's exciting. However, a word of caution here: do not rush to make the hire, even in difficult recruiting times and even during a global pandemic or other business disruption. Doing so may cause more harm than good in the short- and the long-run. (Take a lesson from the Army, where it is often said, "Don't rush to failure.") Stick to the parameters you set at the beginning of the search and do your best not to settle — especially in difficult or uncertain times.

Chapter Eight
Orientation and Onboarding

Onboarding is a popular workplace buzzword and with good reason. Onboarding allows for employees to take some time to get up to speed, helping them to become rock stars at their jobs and really become assimilated into the team, department and company. Onboarding should start with the offer letter, continue through the start date, and keep going for several months until the employee is fully embraced in the job and culture.

Orientation is just a PART of the onboarding process. Granted, it's a pretty darned important part for the paperwork alone! (Thank heavens for electronic onboarding systems — if you don't have one, look into it as a great time- saver on Day 1 of your new employee's career.)

Because so many people use the words "onboarding" and "orientation" interchangeably, there's a huge disconnect in what's needed, what's right, how much is enough, and where to effectively and economically draw the line.

Unfortunately, most "onboarding" for new employees consist of an hour spent with HR filling out paperwork, and from there we send them off with their business cards and say, "go get 'em!" However, when you look at the chart below, you can see we are doing a great disservice to new employees by not giving them adequate time and training to acclimate and thoroughly learn their new position.

Time It Takes a New Employee to Fully Embrace Their New Position

General employee: 6-9 months
Supervisor: 12-18 months
Manager: 18-24 months

Think about the last time you changed jobs and how nerve-wracking day one was. Let's apply that now to building our Onboarding Process. Think: "What can I do, in advance, to help this new fledgling be less nervous from day one and more productive from hour one?" It could be as simple as showing them where they should park when they arrive, talking to them about what people generally wear to work, or recommending where to eat lunch.

The week before new employees start, consider giving them a tour of the building and facilities, including restrooms and fire escapes. (Let's be honest and real here: everybody has to go to the restroom, and nobody wants that to be the first question they ask on their first day.) You might give them a walking tour of the surrounding area, pointing out nearby restaurants and services. You could provide a packet with an overview of the company perks and benefits, a list of the job descriptions, or a chart showing how departments and positions are interrelated. You could also send them training or orientation schedules, so they can ask questions before arriving. The list is almost unlimited — include menus for local delivery restaurants, and Post-It notes on info you send with "this is always a favorite" or "this one is fast." ANYTHING to make them feel part of the team before they even walk in the door.

The more we address the little stuff ahead of time, the more at ease new hires will be when they walk through that door, and the more we can get right into the meat of their job responsibilities on the very first day. Remember, your employees will be getting an orientation from someone. Let's make sure the orientation employees are receiving is accurate and adequate, sending the message the company wants sent instead of the unofficial, water cooler gossip style welcome.

Very little of this will change if you are doing a "virtual" onboarding. Walk through the facility on your video call and "show" people around; send them tips on setting up their home office; provide any "virtual meeting protocols" your organization has established. Find out which restaurants in their area deliver and let them know. (Keep this in mind for future "lunch" meetings — have their lunch delivered!)

The more we address the little stuff ahead of time, the more at ease new hires will be when they walk through that door, and the more we can get right into the meat of their job responsibilities on the very first day.

As new employees acclimate, follow up with them. Ask them how everything's going and listen to them sincerely. Is there anything you could've done better for them that first week? How can you help them be more comfortable next week?

With healthcare and benefits needing to be in place no later than the 90th day of employment, a lot of companies have converted to a 60-day orientation/introductory period to conclude before the benefit-waiting period ends. Having an orientation/introductory period longer than

90 days defeats the purpose of a trial period. Regardless of the length of time, be sure to take advantage of this period. If new employees are right for you, you'll know. If not, move them along or move them out. Be honest. Be real. It's best for you and them.

Items That May Be Included in Onboarding

Post-Offer/Pre-Employment Steps

1. Welcoming offer letter from HR representative; include benefit overview info
   a. Make darned sure their technology/access will be ready for them on day one
2. Email welcome from CEO
3. Email or letter packet from direct manager with parking, dress code, coworker contact info, lunch suggestions (including "hey, a lot of our people pack their lunch and eat together"), or "virtual work" tips
4. Calendar invitation to lunch on Day 1 (send them lunch if they're remote)

Other Ideas

- Welcome sign in the lobby
- Introduction throughout the workplace
- Department meeting — assign a "buddy"
- Time alone to set up their workstation
- DAY ONE: GIVE AN ASSIGNMENT that they can successfully accomplish

Make sure new employees have exposure to all the jobs in the organization, so that they understand how their position fits into the big picture. You can break your orientation down and start with, "Here's our organization, mission, vision, and values. Here's specific

- Follow up on assignment — kudos for any positive effort
- Give coaching also for tweaks — be honest, be real
- Daily check-ins from manager during week one
- Check-in from CEO week two; one-on-one time with CEO?
- Start to detail out specifics of the job description
- Establish expectations
- Discuss training/tools that may be needed
- Monthly check-ins on work assignments and comfort within department/organization
- Regular Q&A sessions with other "newbies"

Items for a Traditional Orientation

- W-4
- I-9
- Benefit Forms
- Handbook
- Organization Chart
- Department Intros
- Here's your desk

information regarding your department. Here's how your department fits into everything." Then break it down even further to, "Here's why your position is important. Here's why you are vital to our success." Make them feel like part of the team.

I think you'll find that your employees will get better at their jobs, faster, if you don't expect them to do everything out of the gate. Instead, walk them through a defined process. Don't just throw them to the wolves, saying, "You've got the job. Go do it."

If you have current employees who were never given orientations, you can still bring them on board. Treat them almost as if they're new employees. Naturally, you don't need to do the new employee paperwork, but you can have staff meetings where you walk them through the onboarding process one section at a time, department by department, and thereby giving everyone a wider sense of the organization.

If your business has a slow period, take employees from one department and have them shadow in another department. Do this for half a day or even just an hour. Let them walk in their coworkers' shoes. Let the warehouse person hear firsthand what it's like when a customer's calling and yelling, "I didn't get my toilet paper today! You sent me paper towels instead of toilet paper!"

So often, I hear supervisors say, "I can't wait until this group turns over and we can start again from scratch." But that's magical thinking. Unless everyone is fired (or quits) on the same day and you hire a completely new team, you never start from scratch. Just like having a starter for sourdough bread, that original culture stays with you. Forever. Fixing the recipe is up to the chef.

⚠ Orientations, Onboarding, and Remote Work – Oh My!

How in the world do you properly orient and onboard someone during a pandemic or a partial shutdown of your business or during some sort of crisis, disruption, or public scandal? You do it carefully and thoughtfully. Because, ready or not, organizations had to begin doing so in March of 2020 and you, too, are going to have to master the art of onboarding during volatile, ambiguous, and uncertain times. Even companies that had great orientation programs before the COVID-19 outbreak had to completely readjust their approach. For companies that barely onboarded staff, it was an almost insurmountable task to get it right and do it remotely. Technology had to be delivered (and set up, in most cases). There were entire companies whose employees were asked to work from home but whose employees didn't have computers or webcams.

So much of traditional orientations and onboarding involve or involved meeting with co-workers and leaders — in the lunchroom, in someone's cubicle or office, on the manufacturing floor, in the hallway. A video "meet" is no substitution from sitting across the table from someone talking about the history of the organization or why the coworker enjoys the work. But it's a good start. A friend of mine has a son who became an engineer for Apple in early 2021 during the height of the pandemic. To date (more than a year later), he still hasn't seen his office or met any of his colleagues in the real world. Not a single handshake. Fortunately, a good deal of his work involves international communications, which would be virtual anyway. But imagine moving to a new part of the country (in his case from Massachusetts to California) and not being able to meet anyone at work or personally? Talk about "disorienting."

These are the new challenges facing employers today — not just during the pandemic, but now and forever. For better or worse, COVID-19 showed how critical a documented, prepared orientation and onboarding system is for the short- and long-term success of employees.

Part Three
Running the Ship

Chapter Nine

Employee Relations

People generally equate employee relations with a union environment. But really, it's about the *philosophy* of your relationship with your employees. What kind of a connection do you want to have? For example, let's say you have an open-door policy about unscheduled meetings and informal communication with leaders, but every time an employee walks down your hall, they see your door closed. What's the real message you are sending?

In regard to any employee-relations philosophy, actions always speak louder than words. I can pull in any number of catchphrases to illustrate this, but it all boils down to *doing what you say you're going to do when you say you're going to do it.* If you say you are going to get back to an employee on such-and-such, then get back to them about such-and-such. And do it relatively soon.

Do what you say you're going to do when you say you're going to do it.

Employee relations also depend upon how you work to gain the respect of your employees. They don't have to agree with every decision you make, but if you have solid employee relations atmosphere in place, they will respect your decisions. Respect is not granted along with your title; it's earned when you consistently demonstrate the mission, vision, and values of the organization. When you live your mission statement daily, you provide clarity in your actions and words. Everyone else will follow suit.

Respect is not granted along with your title; it's earned when you consistently demonstrate the mission, vision, and values of the organization.

Maintaining positive employee relations is a good way to show your employees that you respect them. If they are required to abide by the guidelines you set forth, they need to know that you're going to join them and lead the way. You should be beyond reproach — at least, as much as is humanly possible. And when you make a mistake? "Own" it, be vulnerable, be honest, and apologize — demonstrating your humanity and your humility goes a long way with your employees.

One of our core values at HR Resolutions, my organization, is "going the extra mile for clients is second nature." If I'm not demonstrating this value in every interaction I have with our clients, what message am I sending to my employees? I'm teaching them that they don't have to go the extra mile either. If you want people to come to work on time, then you should be the first one there, greeting your employees as they come in. *You* determine the culture.

Your ability or inability to set boundaries has a huge effect on your employees. If they see you playing favorites, or being especially hard on someone, they are going to do one of two things. They might distance themselves from the pet or pariah, thereby isolating themselves from the problem. Or they might try to insinuate themselves into the relationship, in order to curry favor.

When healthy employee relations are in place, you know to praise publicly and criticize privately. You know when to keep a conversation private and when to celebrate a team success.

Honest-and-real conversations go far with employees.

Labor Relations

Labor relations *do* have to do with a union environment. I've worked in both union and union-free companies, and there is a difference between them. In a union environment, my rules are absolutely black and white. In a union-free environment, my rules are gray. There are pros and cons to both types of environments. If you currently exist as a union-free environment, you'll find one of the most challenging times is when a union first tries to get started in your organization. It is often a time of great confusion and high emotions. Employees are torn between their employer, who they know, and the union, which may be promising the world. As an employer, you're probably angry because some employee sought outside help; you might also be scared because you can't deliver everything that the union is promising. And no one is talking to anyone else!

There is a practice that all managers, supervisors, and leads should learn. It's called TIPS or SPIT — I prefer TIPS because it sounds nicer. If you learn that a union is trying to rally your employees, it's *critical* that you and your supervisors understand these four things:

T – Do not **Threaten** your employees. Don't say, "If you talk to the union, I will fire you."

I – Do not **Interrogate**. Don't say, "Who was at the union meeting last night? Were you involved? Who said what?"

P – Don't make **Promises**. Don't promise things you cannot deliver. For example, "If you vote against the union, we'll give everybody a one-dollar-an-hour raise."

S – Don't do **Surveillance**. If you find out that the union organizers are meeting with some of your people down at the local Elks Lodge, *do not* go to the local Elks Lodge, take pictures of the license plates in the parking lot, and snap photos of who's going in and out.

In all honesty, I understand why certain employers would be terrified of their workers forming or joining a union. On a human level, it makes sense to try to fix the problem by saying, "We'll do better! You don't need a union — we'll fix what you don't like!" But once the union is involved, it's too late. You should've done all that before your employees went and spoke to a third party.

Once you believe that a union is talking to your employees, it is critical that you and your supervisors follow the four points of TIPS. If you don't follow even one of those four points, there is every likelihood that the National Labor Relations Board (NLRB) will come knocking on your door to say, "Congratulations, you don't need to have a union election because you have violated your employees' rights. We've already told the union that they now represent your employees." That's how serious you must take each of the four steps in TIPS.

In all of this, unions are not always a bad thing. They can help your employees organize and clarify their rights and needs, and they can be partners with you — advocating for your employees and speaking up as issues, opportunities, or problems arise. Unions can also make things really difficult for you, especially if you're not being good to your workers. So, follow your best-practice guidelines, and proceed with foresight and care.

The bottom line: Be honest. Be real. If you're fair, consistent, and live by your mission statement, whether employees like or dislike the decisions you make, they will more than likely respect those decisions and give you the benefit of the doubt.

A Word About Employee Relations During a Business Disruption

In all my experience as an HR professional (30+ years), staying ahead of the rumor mill was never as important as it suddenly became at the start of the coronavirus pandemic in 2020. News media, social media, fear, guesswork, and personal experiences all added up to a frenzy of information and misinformation. HR and organizational leaders needed to demonstrate a calm and open approach to employee questions. Even when we didn't know the answers (or when we were scared or when we followed social media too closely), we HAD to be the voice of reason.

When in doubt, the best answer to give your employees is an honest answer. And, if you don't know the answer, tell them that but assure them that you will find out. Employees will truly accept that answer (provided you are true to your word, find out, and communicate fully and timely when following up.)

If information is moving too quickly or there's too much to sort through, as there was initially with COVID-19, consider starting a Frequently Asked Questions document that can be updated by one or two primary staff members and shared throughout the organization.

Be the source of the answers, not the cause of the confusion. You best serve the entire organization with that approach.

Chapter Ten
Payroll

A well-run payroll process is a critical component of keeping your employees happy and feeling like they're in good hands. Besides that, the law requires you to pay people for the work that they've done for you. Your engaged employees might seem like they're working for you for fun, but they're not. There is a paycheck involved.

Take me, for example: I love human resources. I love what we do for our clients. I wish I could give it away for free, but I have people to pay and overhead involved in running a business. My passion doesn't write those checks, and it's the same for your employees. A paycheck is what makes it possible for them to buy food and clothes, to pay the rent or the mortgage, to educate their children, and to commute to the place where they work for *you*. Hopefully, there's enough left over for some fun too.

Sometimes, making payroll work for you means outsourcing it to another company. Outsourcing the payroll takes away a number of concerns that may not be part of your expertise, such as properly calculating tax liabilities. While there is an expense to outsourcing the payroll, you save in other ways — namely, time. Trust me, not having to sit down, figure out, and remit my quarterly payroll taxes is heaven.

Of course, even if you're outsourcing payroll, someone in your organization still must process the paychecks; but personally, I want someone else making those direct deposits. I don't want to be responsible for having to transfer money from my account into four separate accounts for my employees (or 16 separate accounts or 100 separate accounts). I want to make *one* transfer to the payroll company and let their employees deal with it. And if they screw up, the problem is theirs.

Sometimes, making payroll work for you means outsourcing it to another company.

At the end of the day, it really comes down to properly processing taxes and understanding the associated liability. I could pay my accountant to handle it or do it myself; but under those circumstances, I still have liability if it's done incorrectly. And if I'm liable, then I pay any fines, taxes, and penalties. But if I contract with a payroll company to do the taxes and they are done wrong, then that company is liable. It has the responsibility to talk to the IRS, or the local tax representative. That, in itself, is well worth the expense!

Payroll Errors: When Things Go Wrong

Payroll errors happen — after all, you're only human and so are the people who work at payroll processing firms. How you respond and how *quickly* you respond are what matter.

Payroll errors happen — after all, you're only human and so are the people who work at payroll processing firms. How you respond and how *quickly* you respond are what matter.

If you haven't been paying properly, fix it — and fix it before a government agency comes and creates drama you don't want, telling you to fix it (because then you'll be fixing it for a lot more people and for a lot longer). If you make two or three payroll errors in a row, or even close together, employees are going to get worried. They're going to ask, "What else are they not doing right?" That can lead to deeper concerns where they ask, "Is the company in trouble and that's why payroll is messed up or late? What else are they not paying attention to in our company? Isn't this important to them? Am I not important to them?"

The risk of major morale or culture crisis among your employees if payroll is not on time and accurate is another solid reason why it's great to have a payroll service handle everything. You won't be the target if something goes wrong; instead, you'll be helping to solve it.

From time to time, an error is made in your employees' favor, like a larger amount of pay on one of their checks. Contrary to the employees' hopes and dreams, that error does not set a precedent. All errors should and must be corrected immediately.

If an error has been made in your employees' favor, your first thought might be, "Why didn't they notice this and come to me?" Maybe they did notice and kept it to themselves. But it's more likely they didn't notice, simply deposited the check as normal, and moved on. As frustrating as this is, if you didn't notice it, why should they?

As soon as you pinpoint the payroll error, I encourage you to sit down and have an honest conversation with the employee. For example, you could say, "You may have noticed for the last four paychecks, we paid you a dollar more per hour than what we had agreed upon. We can do a couple things here, but I'm sure you would agree that the company needs to get that money back."

Now, brace yourself, because employees are likely to say, "Well, you made the mistake and that money is gone." Take a breath and reply, "Absolutely, we made the mistake, but let's look at it this way: If I had underpaid you by one dollar, wouldn't you want your money? It's the exact same thing on our side. We need that money to pay your coworkers and to help this business grow. I wish we could let you keep that money, but it has already been spoken for in our budget."

At this point, you should come up with a repayment agreement with them. For example, you might adjust their payroll by lowering their pay to one dollar below their agreed upon hourly wage for the next four paychecks to bring things in balance. (This works as long as you're still paying at or above the minimum wage on the reduced salary — you always have to stay true to the wage and hour law.)

Remind the employees that you're not taking anything away from them. It's simply an issue of "We paid you a little too much, and now we're going to smooth it back over. You're not actually making less over the course of the year."

Another thing that happens with some frequency is that an employer under-withholds their employees' benefits. Again, in most circumstances, you are entitled to reclaim that money to pay the associated taxes or fringe benefit premiums. The employees signed up for benefits and understand that there was a cost to those benefits. They have signed an enrollment form that says, "You may withhold x from my paycheck." Therefore, you have every right and responsibility to bring things into alignment.

There may be occasions where you decide to let things go. You may say, "You know what? We're going to let you keep the extra money, not because we have to, but because it's a simple fix. We're going to correct the error going forward and put things back the way they should be."

The main thing to remember is to always have the honest conversation. Don't just make an adjustment or let your employees keep extra funds without telling them why, what happened, and how you're correcting the situation.

Beyond the Paycheck: Total Compensation

While not exactly part of payroll, many of the contributions and deductions included in your employees' total compensation packages are processed through payroll.

We don't talk enough about total compensation. Employees get much more than a paycheck from us. Total compensation is something that we should be singing from the mountaintops. It includes any statutory benefits like workers' compensation, unemployment insurance, Social Security (sometimes known as old age, survivor, and disability insurance, or OASDI), and Medicare.

We don't talk enough about total compensation. Employees get much more than a paycheck from us. Total compensation is something that we should be singing from the mountaintops.

It's good to remind employees that we pay into those government-mandated insurance accounts for them — and these programs *are* insurances. For example, we provide workers' compensation insurance for them at no charge. All we ask in return is that they be safe on the job. You may pay disability insurance so that if they get sick or hurt, you can continue to contribute financially to their household as they heal. At your company, there may be medical, dental, and vision benefits. There may also be paid vacation days, sick days, and more.

It's well worth your time to add what you're paying for all the included benefits you provide and show your employees their percentage of the cost. Explain how the amount you pay is *in addition* to the wages on their paycheck. They may be pleasantly surprised to see how much you're paying to keep them safe and protected.

Supplemental benefits include things like retirement plans and voluntary insurance or other no-cost/low-cost perks. You may choose whether you wish to pay for these additional benefits but many of these are completely employee-funded (except for any retirement funding match), but you should still point out the fact that, as an employer, you make these plans available to them for their choice.

There are also ways that your employees save on everyday things by coming to the office several days a week. These small savings can add up to a big chunk of change by the end of the year. For example, if you provide free coffee in the break room every day, you might be saving your employees a daily trip to Starbucks, you could be saving them $5-$10 a day. Five days a week, 52 weeks a year (minus two for vacation) — that's a savings of $1,250-$2,500, in coffee alone. Add in free lunch on Fridays, at a cost of about $15 per employee, and they save another $750 on lunch. (Okay, for those of us who still go to a brick-and-mortar location. But, what's to say you can't send lunch to a home office? Everyone's favorite restaurant delivers.) Get the picture?

Sample Benefits

Health and Welfare (insurances)

- Dental Insurance
- Flexible Spending Accounts
- Dependent Care Spending Account
- Life Insurance
- Disability Insurance (short- and/or long-term)
- Medical Insurance
- Vision

Time Off Benefits

- Bereavement/Funeral
- Holidays
- Jury Duty/Witness Pay
- Leave Without Pay
- Paid Time Off
- Personal Time
- Sick Time
- Vacation
- Personal Leave

Other Benefits

- Childcare
- Company-Provided Cell Phone
- Credit Union Membership
- Direct Deposit
- Educational Assistance
- Employee Assistance Program
- Matching Charitable Gifts
- Pet Insurance
- Roadside Assistance
- Employee Purchases or Discounts
- Telecommuting

Retirement

- 401(k), 403(b), Simple IRA
- Pension – Non-Contributory

Beyond the break room, there might be company picnics and parties, paid time off, subsidized pre-tax public transportation cards, and use of the copy equipment and paper. All these items add up and are of financial benefit to your workers.

The Devil Is in the Details

A Human Resource Information System (HRIS) is a database that captures any and every piece of information about your employee — age, race, emergency contact information, benefits enrollment, and dependent information, to name a few. Any data that you may need to access on an individual employee can be housed in an HRIS system.

Do you really need a system like that? Depending on the size of your employee population, probably not. If you've already outsourced your payroll, there is probably a field somewhere in that payroll system that is related to whatever data you need to track.

For example, if you need to track gender for some reason, you can bet there's a field in the payroll for an employee's gender. There may not, however, be a field for Equal Employment Opportunity (EEO) classification.

EEO classification is the category or type of work that an individual does based upon nine categories of employment, detailed in the table below.

EEO CLASSIFICATION
0-1, Management
0-2, Professionals

(continued)

EEO CLASSIFICATION
0-3, Technicians
0-4, Sales
0-5, Clerical
0-6, Skilled
0-7, Semi-Skilled
0-8, Unskilled
0-9, Labor

Here's when EEO classifications come into play: if you need to do any type of government work, you may be asked to identify what ethnicities you have employed in each job classification. You may also need to disclose this information if you're applying for any grants, federal programs, or subsidies.

You may also need to track your employees' disability and/or Veteran status, which probably doesn't have corresponding fields in your payroll system. But again, if this status is something you need to track, your payroll company should be able to help you find a category in the system that you can rename (or create a new one) to track this data.

Troubleshooting

Whether your payroll processes are in-house or outsourced, you should audit them periodically using what's called a *gross-to-net test*. Unfortunately, that means that you may have to go to the IRS to get the tax tables and figure out various rates. If that's too much of a hassle, you can do a *thumbprint check*, which is where you take the employee's gross wages and subtract everything that was withheld.

Does it come out to the net amount? If it does, you're done. If not, investigate further.

The reason you go through all this is to demonstrate to an auditor that you pay attention to your payroll. It also helps you check for errors, like accidentally paying someone extra wages. Before you even submit the payroll, make sure that your numbers balance. If they don't balance, figure out why *before* you process checks, when problems are easier to fix. During your internal audit, make sure that your paperwork matches your payroll. For example, if you have an individual marked with "Head of Household" with no additional deductions, make sure that you have the backup of their W-4 that says they've chosen to have taxes withheld in that manner

Depending on the size of your payroll, I recommend that you break it down and audit quarterly to avoid overwhelming yourself.

If an employee wants to change a deduction (for example, if they want to change their tax exemptions or their retirement plan withholding), please don't accept a request via sticky note or e-mail. Make sure they fill out the appropriate form. The IRS audits your tax withholdings and payroll against W-4 forms, and they will not accept an e-mail as a legitimate W-4. You must withhold based upon the legal W-4 document.

HR Insider Tip: W-4 Forms

We use the W-4 as a means to document address changes!

Knowing that payroll — a critical business component — is a well-oiled machine makes your employees confident about planning for the future and trusting that they will be taken care of properly.

A Word About Payroll During a Business Disruption

Payroll is critical during the best of times; it is an employee's lifeblood during an emergency. During the height of the COVID-19 pandemic, some organizations were fortunate to receive grants for "hazard pay." There were other loan and grant programs as well. Some organizations extended themselves in generosity to their employees and provided whatever extra they could to keep people working. Some organizations just were not able to do anything.

Doing what we can for our employees during disruptions is the right thing to do BUT also remember to balance that against the longer-term viability of keeping the business afloat through the disruption — never an easy decision.

Chapter Eleven
Legislative Changes

Managing your business and employees is hard work. Some days, it seems never-ending. Then add to that all the employment regulations you need to be conscious of, as well as any of the regulations that pertain to your particular industry. Factor in your own policies and procedures and processes — and, well, that's a *lot* of rules and guidelines to be thinking about.

Now, let's also add strategic planning, customer issues, equipment breakdowns; I could go on and on. Have I tired you out yet? How about if I give you one worry you can immediately take off your list?

Legislative changes are ALWAYS in the works. Always. Every day. My first book was published in the fall of 2015. Between the book's initial release and the second edition of the book going to press less than five years later (in early 2020), the Fair Labor Standards Act (FLSA) was amended — and then it wasn't. At literally the 11th hour (i.e., on November 30th, when the law was set to go into effect on December 1st), it was put on hold. This was a big one, too — it impacted almost every single employer.

Legislative changes are ALWAYS in the works.

As a reminder, FLSA dictates how a majority of companies classify, and hence, pay their employees. Exempt and non-exempt is defined by the FLSA. **Prior to the legislation being changed**, the "salary" test was set at only $455.00 per week. Generally, if an employee was paid at least $455.00 per week, they could be classified as exempt from overtime pay for hours worked in excess of 40 in the pay week.

The proposed new law would have set the weekly salary threshold at $913.00. WOW!!! If you've done the math, that's more than a 100% increase. Employers were in a panic. Heck, HR professionals were in a panic over this. Trying to explain exempt/non-exempt under normal circumstances is difficult enough. Now, add the fact that the government is "helping" managers with employment classifications, CEOs like me were going nuts. Keep in mind, the salary "test" is not the only test but it *is* the easiest of the tests. There is another way to identify exempt from non-exempt. It is called the "duties test," and is based upon the job tasks of an employee. And, I will absolutely agree, there is a *lot* of gray area when answering the duties test. The salary test is black and white.

Companies went through all the hoops — evaluating jobs, evaluating salaries, making critical decisions that impacted employees. Difficult conversations were held with employees about why, all of a sudden, they had to start punching the time clock even though they had been a salaried employee for four years. (I was not surprised by the number of employees that considered it a demotion.)

Some companies decided it was time to increase their base salaries for their exempt employees (the ones who met the salary test *and* the duties test and were *truly* exempt from overtime). Conversations were held with employees; salaries were increased to meet the deadline for implementation. (The deadline was of course, in the middle of a pay week.) These are the kinds of conversations that everyone likes to hold — "Congratulations, I'm giving you more money because ..."

To this day, I remember sitting on the sofa around 11:00 p.m. at night, scrolling through Facebook. A post pops up about a judge in Texas putting a bar on the regulation. First message — *nah, I'm just not going to look at this until tomorrow morning.* Then, the flurry of posts flooded my newsfeed, so there was no ignoring it. I could not believe what I was reading — do they realize how much work had been done? Are they for real??

6:30 a.m. the next morning, I was texting two of my attorney contacts, saying, "What do I need to let people know? Um, how quick can you get back to me?" By 9:00 a.m., I had a communication out to a majority of our clients that said, basically, "Hey, surprise, um, you don't have to do anything if you don't want to." Almost all our clients had already set in motion and/or implemented the changes. Only one was waiting until the actual last minute. I'm blessed to say that our clients that had already moved forward left everything in place. Not all companies did. Some chose to go back to their employees and reverse salary increases. ☹ The client that was waiting for the absolute last minute to implement the change did *not* move forward and, because we had also not communicated any changes to the employees either, what could have been a source of stress and a major crisis for this workforce was never seen or felt by the employees at all.

What is my lesson in this long diatribe regarding a piece of major employment law that was never passed? *You can't control the legislative process.* Because you can't control it — don't manage to what MAY happen. The above is an extreme example, because the law had passed, and action did need to be taken. But in general, and thanks to the power of social media, we're hearing about legislation that people would like to have passed or have introduced. And depending upon the mouthpiece, we may hear more about one proposal over another.

You can't control the legislative process. Because you can't control it — don't manage to what MAY happen.

Here's my next question for you. Do you *want* to have an impact on the legislation that impacts your business? You *can* make a difference. When I was in my early 30s, I was working for a Division of International Paper. Several members of the various personnel departments were offered an opportunity to learn "Grass Roots Lobbying." We learned how to effectively speak with our legislators, how to write a letter that would get their attention, *and* how to work with the real lobbyists in an effort to support our business needs.

These may not be things you have any interest in doing, but I assure you that your local Chamber of Commerce, or your State Chamber of Commerce, wants to hear from you. They *do* have lobbyists who focus on business and want to hear from businesses. There's also a U.S. Chamber of Commerce — USchamber.com. Get involved — be active in your community and in your state. Honestly, it *does* make a difference.

Get involved — be active in your community and in your state. Honestly, it *does* make a difference.

So, funny story ... Just as I had finished the revisions on the manuscript for the second edition of *Stop Knocking on My Door* (the book that was the inspiration for *Honest and Real*), the U.S. Department of Labor had the nerve to issue the final overtime rule! I know — they did it before but ... In my professional opinion, this one makes more sense and is more doable. The Salary Threshold (or test) is $684 per week. AND it's official and implemented! So — check your weekly pay *and* the tasks that your employees are doing each day. MAKE SURE you are in compliance with the regulations that are in place TODAY (not the ones that MAY be coming!). And, don't forget, your state may have different thresholds. By the way, there are also new W-4 forms and I-9 forms ... yes, sometimes it feels like the changes come every day!

__Nobody knows your business and business needs better than you — effective HR systems can and should include having a voice in the legislation that impacts how you serve as an employer.__

⚠️ A Word About Legislative Changes During a Business Disruption

My head is still spinning. The best thing I could do for my clients at the start of the pandemic was to keep them informed of the vetted and real information that was coming out. I'm not sure of a time when my email was fuller of "newsletters" and "urgent" announcements than March/April 2020. The sad thing? A lot of it was speculation and opinion. For example: I reviewed an e-newsletter from a trusted law firm in our area. The first article asserted that OSHA *would* accept COVID cases as work-related. Further down in the newsletter was another article, prepared by a different attorney of the firm, stating that OSHA *would not* be accepting COVID as work-related. Who do you believe?

As employers and HR professionals, we have a responsibility, especially during an emergency, to find the truth. Turn to your trusted sources — mine were the Department of Labor, the CDC, and the PA Department of Health. Sure, I read all the "stuff" that came in, but I researched as well as I could and then only shared what could be confirmed.

Keep your head about you even when others are running amok!

Chapter Twelve
Benefits Management

As business owners or leaders, perhaps the most important thing to remember about employee benefits is that they don't have to cost an arm and a leg. You've got your traditional benefits like medical, dental, and vision — everybody thinks of those off the top of their head — but there are a lot of other benefits, and they're all potentially valuable in the minds of the employees.

For example, a flexible work schedule is a benefit and may be priceless to some employees. When we interview people for our office and they ask what the office hours are, I say, "We come in any time between eight o'clock and nine o'clock, and we leave any time between four o'clock and six o'clock. But hey, you work from your home office so … as long as the client's happy, we're happy!" Working virtually is a benefit. Offering a flexible schedule — where employees can adjust their own hours — doesn't cost me anything as an employer.

> **Offering a flexible schedule — where employees can adjust their own hours — doesn't cost me anything as an employer.**

When you think about what you might offer outside the traditional benefits, it's smart to ask your employees what they would value. A flexible schedule may not be a good fit for detail-oriented thinkers. They may prefer parameters. A highly creative thinker might love a flexible schedule, but they might need a set schedule to get any work done. Something that's a benefit for one employee could be an irritant for another. It's up to you to find the balance.

You should remain consistent, but that doesn't mean you can't have flexibility in developing a program that's right for both your company and your employees.

Look at your traditional benefits and find an insurance broker who you trust implicitly. This is the person who is going to go shop your benefit plans for you. You want someone who has your best interests in mind *and* knows your market.

You need a broker who is going to help you completely understand cost and coverage differences between one benefit package and another. Your broker needs to understand your mission, vision, and values. Your broker needs to have clarity about your organization, so that they can best represent you out in the benefit marketplace. *They should be a trusted resource for you.*

You should also be able to rely on your broker to help troubleshoot when issues arise. Finding a good broker isn't so different from finding a good dentist, real estate agent, or tailor. Ask around. Trust your peers. Who do they recommend?

If you're unhappy with your current broker, you can always change. I don't recommend that you do so every year, because then you lose any continuity, but it's certainly better to find someone you respect and trust. I get phone calls repeatedly from brokers who say, "Hey, I can get you a better deal." No, they can't. When it comes to benefits for companies with fewer than 100 employees, Broker A, Broker

B, and Broker C are going to get you the exact same rates from Blue Cross Blue Shield or Aetna (or any carrier that works in the under-100 market). The rates are the rates are the rates.

You need to be looking for trust, confidence, and someone you can rely upon. You need to be looking for the cultural fit, and you need to be looking for service. I have some brokers who are completely hands-off. They get you the quotes, you sign them, and they say, "We'll see you next year when it's time for renewal." That's how they are. I have other brokers who partner with me through the entire year. They will come out for open enrollment meetings. They will speak directly with my employees if something goes beyond what I can address. They will be my advocate. They negotiate with my insurance carriers for me.

For example, one of our clients had a plan where there was a 12-month waiting period for major services. That was part of the plan for a long time, but it affected two newer employees when they had to dip into their own pockets. That is contradictory to my philosophy of taking care of my employees. The broker stepped in and renegotiated the plan. It was good timing, because we were just preparing for open enrollment, enabling us to share this with employees in a timely manner. He negotiated to do away with that waiting period, and it only cost us 75 cents per employee, per month. Sometimes, employee care is worth it!

Other partners in providing employee benefits, who are often overlooked by business owners and leaders, are your financial planners. They assist with any retirement plans you may offer. They're not necessarily "brokers," but you want to have someone who is available to speak with your employees, help them make decisions, and describe options to them. That's not something you want to be responsible for unless your expertise is financial and retirement planning.

There are many fiduciary responsibilities you have to your employees when you offer a retirement plan. And it goes beyond legal and ethical responsibilities and more so than any other health and welfare insurance plan, to the point of needing to teach them to use the benefit. You must:

- Provide regular education about retirement.

- Review your overall plan once every three or so years.

- Maintain an investment committee that evaluates the investment funds you are making available for your plan.

Depending upon the type of plan, you have more or fewer responsibilities. With a traditional 401(k), you probably have the maximum amount of fiduciary responsibilities. You are required to audit it every year and evaluate the plan annually. 401(k)s are highly regulated. Based upon the industry, some employers may offer a 403(b) plan; others may offer a Simple IRA plan. Always consult with a trusted financial advisor when making decisions about what type of plan to offer.

The Benefits of Benefits

Offering benefits is one way you can set yourself apart from other employers. More and more employers offer benefits to their part-timers. They want quality workers who stay for years — and they get them. Benefits make a difference with recruiting quality workers and they make a difference with retention.

Benefits make a difference with recruiting quality workers and they make a difference with retention.

The Employee Retirement Income Security Act (ERISA) is the regulatory legislation that protects our employees and their benefits. Imagine withholding money for medical benefits from your employees, but not paying the insurance premiums. Your employees are under the impression that they've had insurance all this time, but when they go to the doctor, their claims are denied because their insurance was cancelled. Or imagine that you've withheld your employees' retirement money, but you never made the matching contributions that you promised, so there's no company money going into their IRAs or 401(k)s. Not only did you fail to remit the money to their retirement funds, but those employees also lost any money they would've earned from interest on those company contributions.

If you've done anything like the above examples, you will be found out. You will get a letter from the DOL (specifically, the ERISA division) saying, "Dear Employer, please help us to understand whatever it is that's going on. *Certainly,* you have not intended to do this, because doing this would be committing fraud." (Sorry, it won't be this nice or comical.)

Besides angry employees, there can be nasty fines and penalties involved. Not only do you have to pay the money that you already withheld (which was they employee's money anyway), but you have to spend time, effort, and energy to figure out the interest that they would have earned, which you must also pay. Finally, you have to pay fines and penalties to the government. That's what happens when you don't pay attention to your benefits. This is not your money to play around with or ignore.

The best companies to work for are differentiating themselves based on employee relations and *perks*. Anybody can offer medical, dental, and vision. Not everybody can (or does) offer flexible benefits. Not everybody can (or does) offer a lending library, or shade-grown coffee in the break room — like Zappos does. Check out fortune.com/best-companies for more innovative ideas that leave an impression on employees — you never know what you may be able to offer that you had never even considered!

The best companies to work for are differentiating themselves based on employee relations and *perks*.

Perks are funded entirely by employers, with no employee contribution. They're not insurance. They're not backed by another company. They're just extra things that we choose to give our employees to set ourselves apart from our competitors, or to align our culture with our mission, vision, and values.

Places like Google and Spotify have perks that seem unbelievable — free meals and snacks, standing desks and yoga ball chairs, nap rooms and game rooms. But the perks make sense when you consider that those companies are looking to draw workers who will think of the office as their home (and will stay there around the clock). While these companies draw different kinds of people, *they each draw the right kind of people for that company.* And not surprisingly, their employees generally *love* to go to work.

Other workplace perks are "offered" by happenstance, like libraries having rows and rows of free books that you can read during quiet hours, before or after work, or on lunch breaks. This is completely free to the library, but it's a big draw to people who choose to become librarians. Find what works for you and what appeals to or even excites your employees.

Common Perks to Consider

- A corner office with windows
- A larger-than-normal office
- A nice ergonomic chair
- A break room stocked with snacks
- Free lunch once a month
- Summer hours
- Permission to bring your pets to work
- Flexible schedule
- Product/service discounts

You may not realize how many perks you're already offering to your employees. Point them out at the next meeting. Be proud. Show your employees that they're getting lots of great stuff, just because you feel like they deserve it and you want them to be happy.

Offering perks can save you time and money in the long run because workplace perks can create workplace satisfaction, which helps minimize your turnover. A little goes a long way.

When we talk about what a good place to work looks like, we're talking about a place where your employees feel protected, plan for their future, and are enabled to care for themselves and their families. With the perks you offer, you may create an environment where your employees have some work-life balance.

One Last Note on Benefits

Remember our discussion on ERISA? Any health and welfare type benefit plan (think insurance — even retirement insurance) covered by ERISA *must* have what's called a Summary Plan Description (SPD). *Not* having an SPD is one of the biggest compliance issues that my colleagues and I at HR Resolutions uncover in the early stages of work with new clients.

An SPD is an official, legal document that describes who has what responsibilities regarding each benefit. For example, who is the plan sponsor? Who should an employee contact with questions about plan administration? The SPD is a summary of the plan document (the legal descriptor of the plan). written clearly and concisely to ensure each individual reviewing it will understand the parameters of the plan. Each plan covered by ERISA (think insurance like medical, life, retirement) should have its own SPD, or you can elect to have a Wrap Summary Plan Description prepared. This is almost exactly what it sounds like ... it "wraps" all your covered benefits into one Summary Plan Description.

And, don't forget your tax-free withholding benefit — this is governed under Section 125 of the Internal Revenue Code (and is often referred to as your "125 Plan"). This is the tax code that allows employers to withhold certain benefits on a pre-tax basis. You are required to have an actual written plan document and SPD of your Section 125 benefits.

These are straightforward documents, but they must be done accurately. There is a cost involved in creating this document, but some brokers and supplemental insurance carriers will do it for free as an added bonus for offering their benefits.

If you aren't sure if you have SPDs and Plan Documents, contact your broker to become compliant as soon as possible (hence, another good reason to work with a trusted advisor!).

As your employees come to understand that you truly have their best interests at heart, the bonds of loyalty and security grow. Overall, benefits management comes down to doing the right thing for the people who are under your care. That's one of HR Resolution's core values: Do the right thing, no matter what. It may not always be easy or cheap, but it's never wrong.

A Word About Benefits During a Business Disruption

Just like payroll, benefits may be critical to your employees during the time of an emergency. We were fortunate in the United States to have COVID-19 testing (and vaccinations) covered regardless of benefit status. That will not always be the case. That does not mean you need to rush out and supply medical benefits for your staff — such benefits are expensive.

However, during the time of an emergency, try your best to help your employees find the support and care they need. Make sure you know the ins and outs of the benefits you do offer so that you can best help your employees maneuver through getting *what* they need *when* they need it.

It's good practice to be an advocate for your employees' health and well-being, whether or not you have the capacity to provide benefits that directly support their health.

Chapter Thirteen
Safety

In this chapter, we'll focus on creating a physically safe environment, starting with company culture and awareness. It may come as a surprise, but 95 percent of workplace accidents are the result of an unsafe behavior (i.e., a cultural problem) rather than an unsafe physical space.

Ninety-five percent of workplace accidents are the result of an unsafe behavior (i.e., a cultural problem) rather than an unsafe physical space.

For example, a file cabinet is not unsafe in and of itself. But if an employee is in a rush and leaves the drawer open, that *behavior* of not closing the drawer creates a hazard. If your employee was feeling rushed, then you have a responsibility to correct the behavior. Perhaps that person has too much work, perhaps they are overstressed, or perhaps there's a busy company culture in place. Maybe they don't understand because you never to talk about office safety. Whatever the cause, you want to create a space where your employees know that they can calmly walk to a file cabinet, get what they need, close it, go back to their desk, and trust that you're not going to be pressing them to hurry up.

Aside from it being the right thing to do, providing a safe work environment is your *duty* as an employer. OSHA's General Duty Clause[1] states that we have the duty to maintain a workplace that is free of hazards.

To do that, you must think like someone who is walking into the environment for the first time. You may be used to that heavy door that swings shut quickly so you've learned how to stop it with your foot before it hits you in the face, but your new sales rep might not know that. Go through your workspaces with fresh eyes (or bring in someone new to walk through the building with you) and fix what needs to be fixed. Ask your employees if there's anything they've noticed, from a sharp corner on a desk that always rips their sleeve, to a slick spot on the floor where the polish is extra slippery.

The best safety program is one that's built on education and awareness.

The best safety program is one that's built on education and awareness. DuPont practically wrote the book on workplace safety programs. There are many programs out there, but you don't even need to invest in one. All you need to do is talk about safety and to have your people talk about safety. If your employees see something that is unsafe, have them fix it, even if it's not in their department. Make it a company policy that if you see a spill on the floor, then you clean it up — even if you didn't cause the spill.

---

[1] OSHA.gov: https://www.osha.gov/laws-regs/oshact/section5-duties

Make sure that your employees know that they can come to you when something is broken, without repercussions. If your equipment isn't working properly, or is broken, or if an employee tells you that something is broken, fix it right away. That might seem obvious, but you'd be surprised how many people just put it off indefinitely with an "I'll get to it later" attitude. That *later* could come when someone gets seriously injured (which is bad enough on its own), and you're in court because you were well aware of the problem.

Fix it early, fix it often. If you wait and a problem gets worse, it's going to cost you more money to fix. But it goes beyond that; it's about a safe environment. I'll once again use my company, HR Resolutions, as an example. We used to have a traditional locking door with a deadbolt. My staff worked upstairs in our building (this was when we *had* a building, before we opted for a virtual office). If I wasn't in the office, that meant the building was left open on the ground level. At one point, when we had an office space for rent, someone walked into the building, went all the way upstairs, and inquired about renting the office space. I had one woman working there at that time, and she was alone. Had the situation been even slightly different — had the person who walked in been someone with bad intentions — she could've been in danger. Within a week, I had a badge entry system and a doorbell installed. Yes, it cost money, but it was my duty to make sure that my environment and my employees were safe.

Training

There are certain safety training programs that should be conducted annually. One is so simple and so much fun that it's hard to understand why employers forget about it: fire extinguisher training. It's a blast, literally and figuratively. It also gives you an opportunity to connect with your community because your local fire department will probably do the training for only the cost of the chemical in the extinguisher. So, not only are you helping the fire department by training your workers to put out fires, you're also contributing to your local fire company. What if your workplace is entirely virtual? Talk to your employees about fire safety at home!

Another training subject that can be a lot of fun is evacuation training. For example, you can have somebody stand in an exit, blocking it and holding a little sign that says, "I'm fire!" I don't care what age you are — you learn better and remember things longer if you are enjoying yourself. Yes, fire extinguisher training and evacuation training are serious business, but you want people to have total recall. To do that, they need to have been paying attention during training.

I don't care what age you are — you learn better and remember things longer if you are enjoying yourself.

As you're doing all this training, you're also passing on your company culture to your employees. You're showing that you take these things seriously, but that you're not there to lecture. You want people to participate and take ownership in the training. I don't know how many office buildings I've visited where nobody moves when the fire alarms go off. People shrug and say, "Those alarms always go off." But someday, there could actually be a fire.

Workers' Compensation

Something employees are uniquely attuned to is *workers' compensation* insurance — mandated insurance, as soon as you have one or more employees, that covers medical expenses, care, treatment, and even lost wages if employees are hurt on the job. Your responsibility will be workers' compensation *management*. If your company experiences a workplace accident, you should investigate it so that you can prevent it from happening again. This is also a time to revisit the General Duty Clause. You have a responsibility to send your employees home whole and healthy. If they are hurt at work, you must make every effort to return them to whole and healthy.

You have a responsibility to send your employees home whole and healthy. If they are hurt at work, you must make every effort to return them to whole and healthy.

History and a lot of studies show that the sooner people get back to their regular routine, the sooner they will recover from a workplace injury. And with all due respect to my attorney friends, you don't want your injured employee at home watching TV and being bombarded with those commercials: "Hurt at work? Call us now!"

In all seriousness, if you want your employees to return to you whole and healthy, you don't want them to fall out of practice while sitting at home, collecting two-thirds of their paycheck. It can be very tempting for them to relax into that kind of routine.

Generally, my philosophy for work injury recovery is that unless you are in the hospital, you come to work. There is always something I can find for you to do, as long as the employee is released to perform light duty work. However, I should balance that mindset against what is in the best interest of the individual healing, and what is best for the safety of other employees.

For instance, if I have someone in a leg cast and on crutches, I don't want that person in the warehouse. But that doesn't mean there isn't work that an injured employee can do. They can help in reception and greet people at the door. I can train them to answer phones or organize files. Whatever it is, I want to keep them an active part of my team. Psychologically, that's healthier for them, and it's certainly better for me to have someone who's pitching in, rather than one who's sitting at home.

When it comes to workers' compensation case management, you want to get involved and stay involved. After a workplace accident, there will be a number of different people involved: the injured employee, the employer, the insurance company, and the treating physician. The insurance company may even assign a nurse case manager to the claim. Everyone should be equally involved in the process. A lot of employers skip out on the workers' compensation process and just let the insurance company handle it, but all parties are best served when employers are actively involved in case management.

A lot of employers skip out on the workers' compensation process and just let the insurance company handle it, but all parties are best served when employers are actively involved in case management.

The more actively you are involved in the case from the start, the less likely it is that an attorney is going to come in. Once an attorney gets involved, you're out. You can still talk to the employee and you *should* talk to the employee about work — they're expected to return to work, and it is your duty to communicate that to the employee, attorney or no attorney — but you cannot talk to them at that point about the case. Saying something like, "Are you satisfied with your provider? Is everything going to your satisfaction?" is off-limits once a lawyer is involved. It's better to manage the case, from start to finish, on your own.

Remember, the adjusters at the insurance company are not necessarily your advocates. They have dozens or hundreds of other injured employees' cases to worry about, and they're looking to minimize the insurance company's costs. Ideally, they will welcome your involvement with the case management because you want to get the employee back to their regular duty as quickly as possible, which saves the insurance company money and takes a case off their docket.

Workers' compensation adjusters get a little nervous when you start saying things like, "You know what? They've been off work too long. I've got to move on." You are not obligated to maintain a position for that person forever. You should follow your ADA and other leave and absence policies. If you have 50 or more employees, you should be putting your injured employee on FMLA. Start that 12-week timer. It doesn't mean that at the end of 12 weeks, you're going to terminate the injured employee; it does mean that at the end of 12 weeks, you get to evaluate your options.

In case management, you should be constantly communicating with the insurance adjuster. Nothing should be a surprise to the adjuster, to the employee, or to you. If you need to move on, you need to move on. It will cost the insurance company more because the employee will be even less motivated to get back to work and will continue to receive their wages from workers' compensation. (So, in the long run it will also cost you more because it will impact your loss ratio and future rates.) But you also can't hold a job for someone for two years — nor should you. All the time you're holding that job, the injured employee may be on your medical benefits program. They're not an active employee, so technically you may be violating your contract with your medical insurance company. There are so many pieces that must be juggled, so it's imperative to manage claims from the start and don't stop until they're resolved.

When You're Honest and Real About Safety

When good safety management is truly in place, you'll see a lot more teamwork among your people. Instead of just managers watching other employees' backs, other employees will watch out for each other and help more often. If you've done things right, your employees are running your safety awareness program for you, saying, "Hey Johnny, you didn't have your seatbelt fastened when you were on your forklift. Gotta buckle up, man!" Your employees will pick up on the education and awareness, and will weave it into their day-to-day behaviors. Repeated behaviors become a matter of culture.

With good safety management, you'll also see a kind of generosity of spirit and awareness that is self-regulating and protective. For example, if somebody's getting a box down off a shelf, a coworker is right there, saying, "Here, let me help you. Let's make sure you're not standing on a rickety chair." Employees have a better understanding of how their actions impact others — they know that if Carla in accounts payable goes down, they're going to have to trust a temp to get those checks out on time.

_____

With good safety management, you'll see a kind of generosity of spirit and awareness that is self-regulating and protective.

_____

What's more, when everything is running smoothly, you'll have a great relationship with your adjusters if there *is* an injury. Make sure the adjusters know that you're there to make their jobs easier. We generally think that adjusters should make *our* lives easier, but you must work together. Just remember — they've got a lot of work on their desks, too. They're just people, and they're people who can really help you when you need it.

An unsafe work environment costs you money in claims, in lack of productivity, and in lack of efficiencies. If you have equipment that's damaged and isn't being repaired, then you have equipment that's not running at its maximum efficiency and most likely creating potential safety hazards as well. If employees have to sidestep safety hazards or spend time *finding* the safe way to get their jobs done, that's wasting time too.

There's a hard cost to maintaining a safe environment, but there's a soft cost too. If you have an unsafe workplace, word gets around. You're going to have a difficult time recruiting and retaining employees. They might come to you for a time, but no one wants to put themselves in harm's way. Conversely, everyone also knows when a company is safe, and they want to work there. Be that company.

A Word About Safety During a Business Disruption

These two go together, don't they? But what do you do when the disruption is microscopic and insidious (like a deadly virus) and not something you can manufacture an environmental correction for or put a machine guard on to abate the problem?

In 2020, 2021, and 2022, employers and employees often found themselves in a debate on the health-and-safety benefits of masking (i.e., facial coverings). Most of us tried our best to adhere to mandates and recommendations, and to do right by our employees and our customers. The debate continues, and I don't intend to answer the debate here (I'm neither qualified — I'm not an infectious disease doctor or scientist — nor am I inclined to go too deep into a topic that has inexplicably crossed into the realm of ideology and politics).

However, remember OSHA rule #1: the General Duty Clause. As employers, we have a duty to maintain a workplace free from harm. If masking, social distancing, and hand washing reduce a risk, couldn't it be argued that we have a duty, as an employer, to enforce those guidelines? As employers, we need to carefully balance the requirements of the law, what's in the best interests of our business, what will keep our employees safe, and what will do the least amount of harm against good employee relations. Then have honest conversations with your employees about the policies you are implementing.

Whether we agree or disagree with mitigations that are put in place for protections at work, it is important to:

1. Know the recommended guidelines
2. Determine the risks associated with various approaches
3. Decide what risks you are prepared to take for your company and your employees.

Chapter Fourteen
Evaluations and Reviews

How do you know when it's time to give someone a promotion? How can you be sure someone's stopped growing in their current position and needs a change? How can you confirm that an employee has reached the critical moment where they need to be terminated? The answer to all these questions is *evaluations*.

Just like you evaluate business (perhaps on a monthly basis when you're looking at your financials), so should you evaluate your staff members. They need to know where they stand. They need to know how they're doing, and so do you.

With proper evaluations, you'll be able to catch problems and nip them in the bud, tweak bad behaviors before they grow to be bad habits, reinforce good behaviors that lead to positive measurable results, and encourage a unified company culture. With steady feedback to your employees and clear goals for their next steps, as well as how they can grow, all of your evaluations can be positive, or at least productive. Doesn't it help when your business evaluation includes what steps you need to take next and what goals you are striving to meet (or exceed)?

Imagine trying to run your business and only looking at your profit-and-loss statement (P&L) once a year — most business owners and CEOs couldn't conceive of that. Now, apply that logic to how you give feedback to your employees. It's no different.

Imagine trying to run your business and only looking at your profit-and-loss statement (P&L) once a year — most business owners and CEOs couldn't conceive of that. Now, apply that logic to how you give feedback to your employees. It's no different.

You wouldn't dream of driving your car for four years without a tune-up, and humans are much more complicated than cars. Long-running Broadway shows deal with this basic entropy by bringing in the director or associate director now and again to hold rehearsals, keeping the actors on track, tightening the dance numbers, and making sure the production retains that opening-night feel. As the "directors" of the productions that are our businesses, we also need to provide that kind of clarity and alignment.

What money do you have available for merit-based increases? What money do you have available for raises in general? What's the going rate for this position? The issues related to performance feedback and compensation, while clearly connected, should be considered in two separate sessions.

Is there a difference between an evaluation and a review? In my opinion, the terms *evaluation* and *review* are virtually interchangeable. To help differentiate between these two terms, you may think of an evaluation as a supervisor *rating* an employee. A review, on the other hand, may be considered a conversation between a supervisor and an employee about where and how things stand. Reviews are

> **HR Insider Tip: Annual Formal Review and Salary Raises**
>
> It's time to break the annual formal evaluation and the yearly raise apart from each other. The review should only be a performance evaluation; it shouldn't be a compensation review. You should do everything in your power to separate those two discussions. When it's time to do a salary review, do a salary review. You should absolutely consider performance in the salary review, but there are other things you need to consider: What's the latest cost-of-living increase? How is the internal equity among staff members and departments?

a little more "feel good." Evaluations are a little more structured and serious, and they fall into two categories — formal and informal.

Informal evaluations are your monthly meetings, your quarterly meetings, and desk-side conversations. Informal evaluations are just that: conversations. "How are you doing? How's this going?" But, they're also course corrections. "Let's make sure we stay on track. Let's make sure we're both on the same page." They're your clarity definers.

Your formal evaluation is your clarity wrap-up. I believe formal evaluations should be done at least once a year. You owe it to your employees to sit down no less than once a year, one-on-one, face-to-face, and say, "Here's how you're doing," and to back it up with documentation and examples to support your rating. You owe it to the business. Again, you don't just look at your P & L once, but you definitely examine it closely once a year when it's tax time.

How specific you get with the formal evaluation is up to you, but it's not unlike an interview. You should have an approach and goals that were planned out in advance.

How specific you get with the formal evaluation is up to you, but it's not unlike an interview. You should have an approach and goals that were planned out in advance.

There are two schools of thought to formal evaluations: either you conduct evaluations, or you don't. I think you should have them, even if you hate doing them. I admit, I hate doing them too, but I practice what I preach. My HR managers and I have monthly meetings (which I implemented with my staff a few years ago), so when we sit down at the formal anniversary evaluation, it should be a no-brainer. (We also schedule weekly "check in" phone calls to ensure we connect, even when we're traveling or in different time zones.)

How and when you review/evaluate your employees is a matter of personal choice. Evaluations take time. It takes time to sit down and discuss things. You may ask, "What concerns do you have? Here's what I've seen. Have you thought about this?"

Ultimately, the more often you meet with your employees throughout the year, the easier the annual formal evaluation becomes. A very important note here: the items discussed on that annual formal evaluation should never be a surprise to your employees.

While monthly reviews are challenging to maintain, monthly check-ins are not. They can be as formal or informal as you want. It's easy to walk the floor and be present, talking to employees, asking how things are going, making mental notes, and keeping track of the general feel of things. These "walkabouts" are a good time to touch base about any safety or time-saving measures and efficiencies your employees may have noticed. It is also a great time to inquire about potential ideas on their minds, or if they feel something could be done differently.

Monthly meetings let me know exactly where my employees stand on their goals for the year. Monthly meetings help them understand me better, too. Being an HR person myself, I can get frustrated that my HR manager doesn't do things exactly the same way I do. But, by having these points of contact, I can better understand and appreciate her methodology and approach. We can work as a team, each drawing from the other's experience and expertise.

If you can't have a five-minute chat with each employee each month, then work out a system where you see everyone on a quarterly basis.

There are two schools of thought on *when* to do formal evaluations: one uses the employee's hiring anniversary date and the other chooses a single time for all the evaluations. My preference is to use the employee anniversary date. Because not all employees are hired at the same time, their evaluation dates are spread throughout the year — maybe two in one month, none the next, etc.

While my preference is to do evaluations on an employee's anniversary date, my actual practice is to do them at the beginning of each year so the employee's goals align with the company's goals. One benefit of conducting all employee evaluations once a year is that every December, for example, you know it's time to do performance evaluations. Keep in mind, though, that if you have a large staff, you could end up with a *lot* of evaluations at the same time. This can lead to less thorough evaluations. With this method, too, you may spend a significant amount of time away from your other work. Based on the size of your staff, find a schedule for evaluations that works best for you, the company, and the employees.

When it comes time to complete an evaluation — its comments and numeral ratings — it's important that everybody understands the form used and its definitions. I always recommend that you have a well-defined scale. *Everyone* in the organization should understand what "meets expectations" means, what it looks like, and what it feels like for each job description. With a solid job description in place, this will help identify if a person is meeting the expected requirements, and if they are performing above, at, or below those requirements. It's right there in black and white.

When rating, I recommend using a scale of 1-5. When you get into using a scale of 1-10, how do you distinguish between a 6 and 7, or between a 3 and a 4? Broader scales can result in diluted and arbitrary feedback. I recommend a combination of numbers and words. I use the numbers to come up with an overall score, and the words to describe the numbers. For example, unsatisfactory, needs improvement, meets expectations, exceeds expectations, and outstanding correlate to 1, 2, 3, 4, and 5, respectively.

Within that scale, I clearly define the difference between "meets expectations" and "exceeds expectations." Everyone should know how someone becomes an "outstanding," or what it means if I give someone an "unsatisfactory." Everyone, including you, should understand the tool before you use the tool.

Everyone, including you, should understand the tool before you use the tool.

During an evaluation, be sure to reference that employee's job description. Remember, we have essential functions, as well as soft skills (competencies) listed in the job description, and should be rating, evaluating, and reviewing people based on these requirements. Essential functions are key but remember — soft skills go into the fit and culture of the organization, and they are just as important.

The Benefits of Reviews and Evaluations

The biggest benefit of reviewing or evaluating job performance is a sense of clarity for both you and your employees. But this only happens when you can have an honest-and-real conversation about performance. If it helps, remember you are evaluating the performance, NOT the person; an honest-and-real evaluation should not hurt someone's feelings. I'm not saying they will jump for joy when they hear how you have honestly evaluated them, but they also should not feel hurt as a person either. I have found that "meets expectations" may feel like a poor review to some employees. It is your job to make sure they understand "meets expectations" is *exactly* what we need and there is nothing wrong with that performance. "Meets expectations" is corporate speak for "good job."

If someone is not meeting your expectations, it is your responsibility to be honest and real about that. Look at it this way — if we can't honestly tell them what they need to do to meet our expectations, aren't we really doing them a disservice? We may spare their feelings, but we won't provide them with the necessary feedback to improve.

Equally important is developing relationships with your employees that are mature and respectful, and that don't have a paternal (parent/child) dynamic. Mature, mutually respectful work relationships are the foundation of an understanding that we're all adults here, this is a business with clear goals, and — while we value each other as people — reviews and evaluations are never intended to be personal. And when people are treated like valued and respected adults, they will behave likewise.

The biggest benefit of reviewing or evaluating job performance is a sense of clarity for both you and your employees.

In providing regular, structured reviews and/or evaluations, you're also showing your employees they have a safety net. They're learning that if they haven't met your expectations this month, there will be an opportunity to spend time together to listen, discuss and understand, so that everyone can move forward with a clear and successful path.

You'll find as you develop a real, authentic relationship with your employees that you will, in turn, build a safe environment allowing for honest and open communication. Of course, if you're stomping around every month, disrupting things and making people feel like you're spying on them, those monthly check-ins can become quite stressful. Make sure there is an open, and honest, exchange of ideas between two adults.

HR Insider Tip: Perfect Timing

The annual formal evaluation is the perfect time to review and update job descriptions. Job descriptions should not be static; they should be fluid. They should be ever-changing, just like your business is always changing, growing, and morphing. The annual formal evaluation is the best time to make sure the job description truly defines the job and to make changes as necessary.

Documenting Throughout the Year

If you don't have a system in place where you're regularly sitting and talking with your employees, I want you to make notes (both positive and negative) throughout the year and put them somewhere safe and memorable. This way, when it comes time to sit down to do the annual formal evaluation, you're not combing through your calendar, trying to remember what happened in the past year or wracking your brain about how well the employee performed a certain task six months ago. With the power of today's technology and calendaring systems, you should be able to find one that works for you

The biggest downfall when preparing yearly evaluations is that we fail to remember the *entire* year when we sit down to prepare the document and we fall victim to what is known as the "recency effect." Human nature is to put the most emphasis on recent history. You should not be relying on your emotions, or your memory, so write notes and keep track of things (both good and bad). If you document an employee's performance throughout the year, you'll have everything right at your fingertips when you go to prepare the evaluations.

Salary Reviews

Most Americans still believe in the Christmas bonus — once a fairly standard thing, it is now basically a thing of the past. Another great American myth is the yearly raise. When it comes to bonuses and pay increases — and please keep in mind, I'm writing from my experience as a Baby Boomer — I was raised to know that my dad got a pay increase each year. That was the American way. But, that's not necessarily the American way anymore.

_____

I was raised to know that my dad got a pay increase each year. That was the American way. But, that's not necessarily the American way anymore.

_____

While I would love to give pay increases every year, I'm not always in a position to do so. In an economy where growth is not always a guarantee, raises and bonuses are very challenging for employers. Instead, I look for other ways to increase value.

For example, instead of providing pay increases one year, we implemented company-provided life insurance, disability insurance, and an employee assistance program. There's a cost to those things, but they also add value. Going back to "total compensation," I make sure that my employees understand the value of what is offered and how

HR Insider Tip: Salary Sites

Avoid sites like Salary.com when you are trying to determine pay ranges and what's "right" because they are compiling data from a company the size of HR Resolutions to companies with thousands of employees in non-profit, profit, manufacturing, professional services ... get my drift? *Your* situation is nothing like everyone else's situation. What you *can* do (and HR Resolutions' absolute fave spot for wage info) is head over to onetonline.org (O-Net OnLine). There's no charge; it includes data from occupations, gives you recommended skill sets, and a whole plethora of information down to your *local* metropolitan statistical area — HR speak for your market.

that contributes to their bottom line. I'm not secretive about that because I don't want them to say, "Oh, I didn't get a raise this year." I want them to be able to say, "My compensation package improved this year."

There are many other types of rewards that you can offer that don't cost an arm and a leg. It's sometimes just a simple thank-you to an employee, spoken aloud, or written in a personal card. At HR Resolutions, our employees know that if we hit a certain revenue level quarterly, we do something fun. For example, mimosas and mani/pedis in the middle of a workday! My employees get to choose the "fun," so I don't need to worry about someone *not* wanting to go. Mani/pedis (for example) are not something paid directly to the employee, so they will not be taxed on it. Frankly, it's a tax write-off for the employer because it's a team-building day and a business expense.

Let's be honest, though: changing only benefits doesn't help pay the bills for your employees ... money matters. From a human perspective, you want to recognize that your employees' costs are increasing just like your costs increase, so you need to be sensitive about making sure that you're paying a respectable, livable wage. That means you want to make sure that you are paying comparably to other companies in your area (rather than just those in the same field of business). When it comes to jobs, you're recruiting against all the other companies in your area. You want to do what you can to retain your employees. Pay the best you can and be honest and real with your employees about it.

Find out what's important to your employees.

Find out what's important to your employees. Do they want more education? Do they want to attend a seminar or professional development workshop? A seminar could benefit the work they do for your company, but if you don't pay for it, their only options are skipping it or paying for it out of pocket. It makes sense to add these things to your employees' total compensation packages.

I know of a company that is located above a fitness gym. The CEO got a corporate account at that gym and offered membership to her employees. Not only did this reinforce wellness and provide stress management, it showed that the boss was listening to them when they were talking excitedly about the new (and expensive) gym downstairs.

Professional memberships — in trade associations or other membership organizations — can be very important to your employees' professional growth and development. They're a good way to be recognized within your industry or profession. If you run a marketing agency, consider paying the annual dues for employees who want to participate in the American Marketing Association. Company-paid employee memberships in industry associations is a type of reward and is part of the total compensation package you offer when bringing someone on board. While there's a cost to memberships, you're also increasing the value of your employees by providing them additional professional education and exposure, so it's a perk you benefit from too.

Whichever pay approach you take, you must be consistent. Make sure you can compete against other businesses and organizations. This means playing and paying fair.

When an Employee Asks You for a Raise

One of the most awkward work-related meetings is when an employee surprises their employer by asking for a raise, often doing so out of the blue. I usually respond with a version of, "I appreciate you bringing that to my attention. Tell me what you're thinking and why you deserve a raise." (I'd probably respond a little more softly than that, but if someone wants a raise, I expect that person to tell me, quite frankly, what's in it for me.) I always make the asker do the work. Employees asking for raises need to be able to explain what they've done for the business. It can't just be a matter of wanting or needing more money. If that was the case, we'd all get raises every day!

Here's an example of a meeting that makes sense: Say my marketing manager asks for a meeting. Then he shows me that he saved the business 30 percent on print ads this year and brought in an additional $20,000 of business through relationships he nurtured with trade association contacts. Looking at that data, I would say, "You're right. We should look at that." The employee is redefining the position through his hard work. I should respond by taking the new situation into consideration and reconsidering the value it has to the business.

If it becomes clear during the meeting that the employee just wants more money, I typically respond, "I get it. I want more money, too. But I can't get more money until we have more sales, so go get us more business, and I'll get you more money. That's how we can work together to make this happen." This takes a potentially negative situation, makes it a proactive plan for change and improvement, and the employee leaves with clear parameters of how to reach that goal. I might also say, "You're in this professional association that we pay for. Are you talking to them? Are you introducing our products and services to them? I'll tell you what. If you can get us three new pieces of business out of that professional association in the next year, we will consider a commission, bonus, or other means of compensation." On a side note, do NOT say this if you won't honestly and truly consider doing so.

Before employees leave this kind of meeting, they should have a clear understanding that they must contribute to the company and help it to grow. That's how we find and justify more money for salary increases.

Workplace Coaching and Counseling

Coaching and counseling are vital reasons to have conversations with your employees throughout the year. Just the two words themselves conjure up different pictures in your brain. *Coaching* is like mentoring, where we're developing our team and putting training in place to make them better. *Counseling* is offering guidance by empowering an individual to accomplish a goal or helping them to resolve a conflict. The two are still very similar, and we should be looking at any counseling as coaching.

The bottom line is that we want people to maximize on their full potentials and do their jobs both successfully and happily. Taking time to advise, coach and counsel your team members, allows space for both parties to identify any or all issues at hand, and to mutually clarify how and what must be done for those team members to reach success. Granted, if I have the same coaching conversation a couple of times, I'd better change over to counseling mode. In that case, I'd say, "We're having this conversation again because you have not demonstrated your understanding of the expectations that we established the last time we spoke."

During an initial counseling conversation, I usually fall on my sword and ask the employee whether the lack of clarity was my fault for not explaining it well. This next sentence is going overboard, but I may say, "I must not have explained myself well. Let me help you understand *why* it's important to come to work on time. 8:00 a.m. is when our workday begins, and our customers start to reach out to us for assistance. Everyone else is here, and you need to be here, too. For clarity's sake, our starting time is 8:00 a.m. I'm going to write down that I told you that our starting time is 8:00 a.m., and you can initial that you understood." If they say that they're having trouble waking up, we start to brainstorm ideas that may help them better manage this situation.

Melodrama aside, if we change our mindset on disciplinary actions and think of them as coaching opportunities, we can accomplish so much more. Our employees will start to trust us as well, and they'll be more likely to seek us out for coaching and mentoring on their own. They may come to you and say, "I'm having trouble understanding the need for this new policy. Can you help explain why it's in place? Can you help me determine my priorities with this change?"

If we change our mindset on disciplinary actions and think of them as coaching opportunities, we can accomplish so much more.

As always, all evaluations of employee performance and behavior should come back to clarity, accountability, respect for the employee, and respect for yourself as a business owner. When evaluations are done correctly, everyone moves up the ladder together.

A Word About Reviews and Evaluations During a Business Disruption

Just like interviewing, we needed to learn a new way to talk with our employees. While no one (generally) likes doing reviews, a global pandemic may have made them seem less important in the short term. When it comes down to a choice between making decisions about the survival of the business or completing a performance review, well …

If you need to "put a pause" on reviews for a period during or immediately after a business disruption, by all means — do that. But be sure you communicate that to the employees AND have a plan in place for "catching up." Reviews and evaluations are an important part of being a leader and an employer. If someone is or is not meeting our expectations, we should let them know — even in times of crisis. Have an honest- and- real conversation about expectations.

And if someone is violating a policy or posing a risk to the organization? There is no waiting. We still must do our jobs as leaders and have "counseling" discussions with employees. If nothing else, be sure to send a "recap" email or memo to memorialize the conversation you had.

Keep moving forward but, even in an emergency, we should still be holding ourselves and our employees accountable.

HR

Part Four
Parting Ways

Chapter Fifteen
Terminations

This chapter will cover the difficult but vital topic of terminations and how best to handle each situation.

When coaching and counseling don't work, it may be time to consider termination. It's okay to say, "You're fired." Sometimes, the reason we don't terminate people is that we're afraid of being sued or because we don't want to hurt their feelings. You don't want to be the reason that someone loses the means to make money and feed their kids. But remember this: if it's not a good fit, then it's best for *everyone* involved for the misery to come to an end. The longer you let an untenable situation go on, the worse things get, the more miserable the individual gets, the more customer problems arise, and the more the proverbial cancer spreads to the employee's coworkers. Don't forget that by not terminating someone, you're also preventing the right person from being able to step into that job.

You have a responsibility to the whole. If you have a bad apple, get it out of the barrel before it spoils the bunch. That happens in apple barrels *and* in organizations. If your good employees constantly see a less-than-stellar employee getting away with unreasonable behavior or poor performance, they may flip sides and become disgruntled and dissatisfied employees themselves. Why should they be busting their buns when Joe sits in his chair all day listening to music? It won't take long before they decide that they, too, shouldn't have to work so hard.

You have a responsibility to the whole. If you have a bad apple, get it out of the barrel before it spoils the bunch.

Let's refer back to coaching and counseling, as well as the title of this book, *Honest and Real*. One of three things is going to happen when you give somebody a disciplinary notice:

1. That person is going to step up, pay attention, and improve. (That's a good thing.)

2. That person is going to give up and resign, removing themself from the situation. (That's also a good thing.)

3. That person is not going to change, and you're going to be able to remove them from the situation, properly. (This, too, is a good thing.)

Only one of those three things will happen; but in the end, they're all good things.

Hire Slow, Fire Fast

When it comes to having the law on your side, keep in mind that there's a difference between having a bad attitude and exhibiting bad behavior. It is difficult to fire someone for being negative. The attitude is annoying and might warrant some coaching but it may not be truly "actionable" from your vantage point until they start exhibiting that negativity in communications with customers and/or coworkers.

That combative communication is the *behavior* associated with the *attitude* of being negative. You're not terminating people based on an attitude. You're terminating based on a behavior that has been clearly and thoroughly documented.

Many times, a supervisor will call HR and say, "I am going to fire Tammy today." The HR manager (99.9% of the time) responds, "Okay, where's the documentation?" The supervisor replies (99.9% of the time) that they don't have any, but they've had problems with Tammy for a year. The HR manager replies that Tammy has exceeded the boss's expectations for the past four performance evaluations. Here's where you need to choose the risk level you're prepared to take — you can spend time coaching and documenting, or you can cut to the chase.

And this all matters because it matters to your state's department of unemployment security (i.e., "the unemployment office"). Unemployment often looks at the incident that caused the termination — the straw that broke the camel's back, if you will. What happened?

There are times when it is absolutely appropriate to make an immediate termination, and those things should be crystal clear in your handbook. Obvious grounds for immediate dismissal include theft from the company, coworkers, or customers; sabotage of equipment; threat of bodily harm; and physical violence. For most other things, especially performance-related matters, regulatory and unemployment agencies are going to look for proof of progressive coaching and counseling, as well as for the documented moment when you specifically told that employee, "If you do this again, you will be terminated."

Being able to make that call goes all the way back to the center of the HR wheel — job descriptions — and carries right on through the recruiting and hiring processes. Of course, try as we might, no matter how carefully we prepare our questions and consider our candidates, we all make a bad hire occasionally. I don't care how long you've been doing this, or what your track record is … it's bound to happen.

As soon as you recognize that you have a bad hire, remember, "Hire slow, fire fast." Unless you're a masochist, you're going to want to get that person out quickly! And honestly, keeping a bad hire around puts you into uncomfortable territory because you're torturing your other employees, your customers, yourself, and even the individual who isn't a fit.

The best thing to do with bad hires is to let them go be productive and happy (or lazy and miserable — it's up to them) somewhere else. Wish them well. Have courage and let them go. And whatever you do, don't "lay them off." If you say you're laying them off (inferring there is a lack of available work) but turn around and hire someone else for the position next week, you could be facing a lawsuit for your actions. It's best to sever things based on the real, job-related reason.

The best thing to do with bad hires is to let them go be productive and happy (or lazy and miserable — it's up to them) somewhere else.

I would be absolutely remiss if I didn't suggest that you seek legal counsel anytime you have a termination that feels like it falls into a "gray area" and/or one that involves a "protected class" situation (e.g., age, gender, race, creed, color, national origin, Veteran status, or any other category protected by law). Remember, it's still okay to terminate, as long as it's not for a discriminatory reason (and this is one of the many reasons *why* all that documentation is helpful!).

Unemployment and References

Unemployment is an insurance fund. You've been paying into it, so it's okay to use it. That's what it's there for! But when someone resigns or says that they quit, it's critical to get that voluntary resignation from the person signed, dated, and in writing. Without that record, someone who quit can easily claim that they were fired and are entitled to undeserved benefits.

In all honesty, unless you have a lot of terminations, unemployment claims really don't hurt at all. Think of unemployment as a big pie: You're paying into the state's pie fund, as is your employee. Your company is assigned a slice of that pie — X percent of that pie belongs to you and can go to people you've terminated. As long as you don't take a bite out of somebody else's slice of pie, then one claim has very little impact on you. You haven't exceeded what you've paid in.

But if you have a ton of turnover and go outside of your little slice of pie, then in future years you'll be responsible for paying for a larger slice of the pie, as well as paying back the extra pie you "ate" the year before.

While there are unemployment claims that you can avoid, there are a number of situations where unemployment is a completely valid and useful insurance to help and protect your workers.

If you must cut hours or conduct a true organizational restructuring where you're moving positions and responsibilities around, you may be faced with doing layoffs. When you tell people that they're being laid off, it's almost guaranteed that they're going to get unemployment. As I said, never try to soften the blow of a termination based on performance or conduct by telling someone that they're being laid off. You have less protection against unemployment being claimed, and you fail to sever the tie between you, your company, and your soon-to-be-ex-employee.

Never try to soften the blow of a termination based on performance or conduct by telling someone that they're being laid off. You have less protection against unemployment being claimed, and you fail to sever the tie between you, your company, and your soon-to-be-ex-employee.

If people truly believe that they've been laid off, they may also expect you to bring them back at some point. Unless you are really in a lay-off situation and planning to reintegrate them, it's best to terminate.

When you're in a termination meeting, one of the things that can help is to talk about unemployment and references. Aside from how terminated employees are going to pay their bills, these are two things that will be foremost on their minds. Help lower their stress and fear by walking them through the process of how it's going to work. Don't make any promises and be sure to let them know that the employer does not decide eligibility for unemployment compensation benefits.

Whether someone is granted unemployment benefits is not your call. I typically explain, "The unemployment office is going to send me paperwork. I have a responsibility to complete that paperwork truthfully, but the decision about whether you receive unemployment pay is not mine. The local unemployment bureau decides if you qualify or not."

When people lose their jobs through no fault of their own, they are generally eligible for unemployment. Here's the frustrating part, from an employer's standpoint: "through no fault of their own." One would think that coming to work late every day is within a person's control.

One would think that if someone continues to make errors when inputting customer orders, then that would be the person's fault. Not quite — it could be seen as a performance issue. Did you complete process training? Retraining? Counseling? I hope so, because the hearing officer is going to ask the individual, "Did you perform to the best of your abilities?" I guarantee that the person is going to say, "Yes, I did, but their expectations were way too high." Based on that statement, the former employee's failure was outside of their control. If the hearing officer agrees, then you're out of luck.

While it can be frustrating to think that the person who just stole from you due to all the errors they made in customer orders for six months might get unemployment benefits, sometimes it's best to just do whatever you can to speed the process along so the trouble goes away. Then you can get that person out of your life and out of your company.

Another common trap is the attendance issue. If a company uses a points (or demerits or any number of names) system, then on the surface, it seems fair. If you are late, you get so many points. If you're absent, you get so many points, no matter the reason. When you reach a threshold of X number of points, you're terminated. But unemployment is only going to look at the last event. If that last event was the result of an accident on Route 95, that individual instance of tardiness was outside of the individual's control, and they're granted unemployment — even though the other 20 times they were late were because they slept in.

If you don't care whether or not the person gets unemployment, you can simply write, "Employer has no desire to contest" on the unemployment claim form. With that, you're basically telling the bureau, "You make the decision, I'll run with it." In the event that the employee is denied unemployment, and they appeal, if you don't wish to challenge the application for benefits, don't go to the hearing. That way, the hearing officer only gets one side of the story, and because it's the employee's side, the decision is typically reversed.

More problematic than a layoff is a forced resignation. While you might offer someone the opportunity to resign in order to save face (and avoid a lawsuit), it's not uncommon for a supervisor to try to force an employee to resign in order to avoid an unemployment claim. The supervisor may even succeed in bullying or pressuring such people into saying that they resigned, even though they would have been fired if they had stayed. When the unemployment claim comes, the employer responds that the employee resigned. But if the employee can demonstrate that they were going to be fired had they not resigned, that will be considered a situation outside of their control, meaning that they qualify for benefits. (HR terminology: constructive discharge!)

As I mentioned, another thing that helps cool down a termination meeting is to go through the company policy on giving references. Let the person being terminated know that if people call for references, you only share X, Y, and Z. You won't tell callers the reason for the separation, or anything else that could keep the person from future gainful employment. Remember, you should not blacklist anyone, no matter how much you might want to.

When those reference check calls do come in, be careful and truthful. If you can't say something nice, don't say anything at all. Or, find the one good thing the person did, and focus on that. For example, no matter what question they ask you, answer with, "They came to work on time." The caller should pick up on that tactic and read between the lines.

One question you're almost always asked is, "Would you hire so-and-so again?" I wouldn't answer yes or no, unless I have the documentation to back up why the person would not be eligible for rehire *and* a signed release. You could also say, if it's true, "Our company policy is that if someone is terminated, they're not eligible for rehire. If someone does not give proper notice, they're also not eligible for rehire."

We had a termination that took place after an individual threatened the company in front of a vendor, saying he was going to come back and shoot up the whole place. We take threats very seriously. There were no write-ups leading up to that incident, but his threat was grounds for immediate termination.

Because the employee worked in a shop with heavy equipment and tools that could be used as weapons, we called the police to be present during the termination. As we approached, I had the manager remove his tie because I feared it could be used as a weapon.

When we arrived, we called the employee outside of the shop where we were waiting with police in the background. The employee walked out of the shop with a tool in his hand — something with a weird little hook on it. Playing dumb, I said, "Oh, that's an interesting little tool. Can I see that for a minute? What's it do?" He handed it over to me, and I put it behind my back so that I could drop it if I needed to, in case he went for me.

We took those precautions to protect ourselves, our coworkers, and the employee himself. Afterward, we also put the facility on an immediate lockdown for 48 hours for a kind of cooling-off period and had the police make extra patrols through the area. In most cases, terminated employees are angry, sad, and scared — even raging and out of control — but they generally cool down within a couple of days and begin to move on.

It's very, very rare that a former employee will come back for physical retribution. However, the possibility is there — you've seen it on the news — but how *often* do you see it on the news, compared to how many employers are out there in the United States, hiring and firing people daily? That tells me that it rarely happens and that the chances of having it happen to me are very, very, very slim.

Beyond Common Sense: Protective Measures and Proper Files

I always recommend that you keep former employees' personnel files through your open tax year but check your federal and state regulations for rules on record retention. There are statutes of limitations on when you can be sued through the regulatory agencies or the individual. The maximum is generally two years, so you want to keep files for at least that long.

If you catch wind that somebody is considering suing you, lock down everything. Keep it all — that includes electronic communications — which can be obtained through what's called e-discovery.

Even the meekest employees can turn on you once you've let them go. They may stuff a couple of pens in their bag to show you who's boss, or they may clear the entire contact database on their computer and delete all the marketing files.

If you know that you're going to let someone go, you'll want to have a plan that's set and ready to go with whomever handles your IT. For example, my IT is outsourced, so as I head into the meeting, I'll send a text, "Meeting now." Because I've told them ahead of time that this was going to be happening, they know it's time to change the passwords on that employee's e-mails and disable remote access.

After terminating people, do not let them go back to their desk or computer. And because most work e-mails can be accessed from smartphones now, IT should already have changed their password.

The person who has just been terminated should not be left alone in your environment, but you also must be cautious of a civil suit for intentional infliction of emotional distress. I guarantee that anytime I've walked somebody to their desk and hovered, the rest of the office knows that person has been fired. Be as discreet as you can, while still protecting the company. Still, when I take people to their desks to clean out their personal things, I have a duty to make sure that it's only their personal things they're taking.

An alternative is to say, "We need you to leave the building now, but would you like to come back tonight after hours to get your things?" Or, "I can meet you here tomorrow, before the building opens." If that's not a viable option, say, "We will pack up your personal belongings and ship them to you."

Terminated employees often ask, "What about my personal contacts and e-mail?" Your response should be, "We will go through your contacts and send you those that are obviously not company related." If they ask to get them now and say that they don't trust you, you answer, "I'm sorry, your computer is company property." Remember, no good deed goes unpunished, so don't get sucked in.

What you *should* do is make sure that any documentation you need to give the employee has been prepared ahead of time. Make sure that you're prepared when you go into termination meetings. You should know what you're going to say, what you need to tell them, and what you need to get from them, including any passwords, keys, credit cards, and technology. Be in control of the situation from the first moment. Be prepared to have their technology cut off while you're in the meeting. Know exactly who is going to execute what steps. Know where their e-mails are going to go and where their phone calls are going to be directed. The more proactive measures you have in place, the better prepared you'll be for the unexpected.

Make sure that you're prepared when you go into termination meetings. You should know what you're going to say, what you need to tell them, and what you need to get from them, including any passwords, keys, credit cards, and technology.

When it comes to sharing the news of the departure with your other employees, again, prepare what you're going to say ahead of time. In my experience, less is better. It's perfectly reasonable to say, "So-and-so is no longer with the company." End of story. Some may choose to reach out to the former employee to get the scoop, but most won't. Either way, it's not your problem.

Terminations and Levels of Volatility

If you expect that someone is going to take a termination badly, you'll want to consider a few options. Can the termination take place outside of the office? Are you able to do it in the morning, before anyone else comes in? Can it happen after work hours, when people have gone home? In deciding this, you also need to think about protecting yourself.

If you believe that it's going to get violent, there are some definite steps you should take. Sit closest to the door, so your exit path is clear. Have someone outside the office or conference room ready to dial 911. If you are seriously concerned, you may want to have a police officer and/or security guard present. In a volatile situation, you should not have anything nearby that could be used as a weapon; this includes pens, staplers, and paperweights.

If you're in a termination meeting and someone starts yelling and or acting in a potentially threatening or disruptive manner, shut them down immediately. If the behavior continues, say, "This meeting is over. You either need to exit the building or I can call the police." Usually, they're yelling because they're angry, and they're angry because they're disappointed, hurt, and scared. Mentioning the police may snap them back to reality. In that case, they'll generally do what you ask.

If they *don't* stop yelling or if they begin to threaten you, then end the meeting and ask them to leave immediately. Then, if you have a security officer or department, call them. The important part is to remove yourself from any danger and get the terminated employee out of the building.

Terminations are difficult but can usually be handled in a professional manner. The worst we want to happen is an unemployment claim, which is fine. You pay into that insurance anyway. Keep in mind, the terminated employee(s) may sue you. I say that very nonchalantly, but in all honesty, people can sue you at any time for any reason. These are certainly both better than to be hit in the head by a big metal stapler.

As a precaution, you should explore employment practices liability insurance (EPLI). EPLI is an insurance policy specifically covering many employment practice lawsuits. If sued, you pay a deductible, but the insurance takes care of the defense, fines, penalties, charges, and the settlement. It's well worth the money. I have it, even with only four employees. If you have done your due diligence and you have documented everything, then the only thing is the nuisance of the time, effort, and energy it's going to take.

HR Insider Tip: Never Fire on a Friday

"Never fire on a Friday" — this is an old adage from back when people had to physically go into the unemployment office and file for benefits. Even though you can now file for unemployment 24/7, I still follow that "never fire on a Friday" rule. And here's why … You don't want people stewing for two days before they walk into the unemployment office or attorney's office. If you fire people on a Friday, all they may do is sit around and drink vodka, kvetch with their friends for two days, and get all riled up. It's better to fire people early in the week, so they can calmly get things in order.

Terminating Via Zoom

Ugh, never recommended if you and your employee live in the same general geography; terminations, when possible, should be face-to-face, not over video. I won't even say it's a new reality — lots of companies have had staff outside of their immediate "home" office area for years or even decades before the pandemic. You would never call an employee into corporate and say, "By the way, um, would you bring all our company property with you?"

When terminating virtually, honestly state that you wish you did not have to deliver this news in this fashion, but you believe it is actually in the employee's best interest. (You certainly wouldn't want me showing up at your front door.) Be sensitive to systems cut-off — you don't want IT cutting them off in the middle of your conversation. But it is a significantly more difficult dance than meeting in person. Timing and coordination is everything.

Terminating an employee is one of the most stressful situations you'll have at work, but with good planning and documentation in place and an exit strategy ready to go, you'll be ahead of the curve.

⚠️ A Word About Terminations During a Business Disruption

Compound an emergency, crisis, or other disruption with a concern about the viability of your business during the emergency and you have a hotbed of emotions. The owner, the employees, the HR department, the leadership — all are on pins and needles.

What can you do? I'll use one of our clients as an example. Their company was more than 40 years old and had *never* had a layoff or downsizing before. Almost the minute that the President of the United States closed businesses down for two (2) weeks in March of 2020, the company lost a third of their business — immediately! The difficult decision was made to reduce the staff by a third as well. Across departments, across divisions, across segments — all managers had to determine who stayed and who went.

Because we moved quickly, the rumor mill was held at bay. All the eliminations happened on the same day to further reduce the rumors that went around. What else did we do?

- All managers were coached and given their talking points
- We waived our "no payout" of unused vacation and were as generous as possible
- Individual reference letters were supplied to each employee
- The various unemployment offices were contacted at the same time by HR

Did it ease the situation? Only somewhat because, of course, the situation was horrible. But we were able to demonstrate we were doing everything possible for our employees even if we had to put them in a layoff status. (The company also went on to "pivot" how they went to business, and they were able to replace a good deal of the lost business via new avenues of selling, which led to new positions being created before too long.)

Chapter Sixteen
Resignations

There are two kinds of reasons for a person to leave a company: involuntary reasons (termination, restructuring, and layoffs) and voluntary reasons (resignations and retirements).

Whenever employees voluntarily leave the company — even with resignations and retirements — you want to get it in writing. If they will not give you anything in writing or if it just doesn't make sense for them to do so, then send them a letter stating, "We accept your voluntary resignation, given to so-and-so, on such-and-such date, effective on such-and-such date." You want that documentation on hand in the event they file for unemployment in the future.

Here's an example. An employee leaves your company to go to another job. That person's new job doesn't work out, so they have been fired from the new job and are now eligible for unemployment. However, that person didn't work with the new company long enough to have a stake in that company's slice of the unemployment pie. Where is unemployment going to search? *Your* slice of the pie. Except you have that signed document that states the person in question left voluntarily. Therefore, that person can't access your pie. This is called "relief from charges." You want to ensure you have a written resignation so that you can request this "relief" now and in the future.

Then there are crazy days when somebody decides to yell, "I quit, I quit, I quit," and storms out. You can follow that dramatic episode with a written letter stating, "We accept your voluntary resignation given in the break room on June 9th." The person may come back and reply that they didn't mean it. With that letter in hand, you are then able to respond with documentation and a clear explanation of the events that led to the individual's determined voluntary resignation.

HR Insider Tip: Perfect Timing

Some states require that earned, unused vacation days/hours should be paid no matter what, even if someone quits or is fired. Be sure you know your state wage guidelines.

Make sure that your company policy doesn't *require* a notice period. You may be in an *at-will* state, which means you can terminate an employee at-will (i.e., at your discretion), and your employees can leave employment at-will, with, or without notice

You can *request* notice, but if you *require* it, then you may be required to give it too, possibly giving up your at-will employer status — and, believe me, you don't want to do that. You want the right to let someone go on the spot, if necessary. Most employees will give you at least a two-week notice as a matter of courtesy, but don't expect it, unless you are prepared to give your employees notice in every situation.

There are instances where employees will wait until the very last Friday before they start their new jobs to tell you that they're not coming back. You may want to think about why they do this. Were they worried about retribution? Did they feel so uncomfortable talking to you that they didn't want to deal with a possible confrontation? Do they simply hate working for you? Whatever the reason, they're gone now. Make whatever adjustments you need and move on. If this is happening a lot in your environment, this adjustment *may* mean looking in the mirror; have an honest and real look at yourself as an employer. (Keep in mind, if a new employee is coming to work for you without giving notice to their last boss, take note. That person may end up doing the same thing to you when they are ready to move on!)

As employers, we have the right to accept employees' resignations, effective immediately. We don't have to accept the terms of their notice, and we don't have to pay them for days past the day they resign (unless we let them keep working, obviously). If someone gives you two months' notice, it's your right to say, "That's okay, we accept your resignation effective today."

However, if you go that route, keep in mind that you may have some exposure to unemployment claims for the time between the day you terminate such employees and the date they offered as their last when they gave notice. Using that formula, if they give two weeks' notice and you say, "You can go today," then you have effectively removed them from work for two weeks through no fault of their own. After their two-week notice period is over, they would no longer be eligible for unemployment. Two weeks of unemployment may be worth getting these employees out the door, especially considering that there's always a one-week waiting period with unemployment. Do not offer to pay someone through their notice period as an incentive not to take unemployment. People can take your generous offer of continued pay *and* receive unemployment benefits, because the State still considers them unemployed through no fault of their own during that "resignation" period. So unless you want them to get unemployment *plus* the two weeks of salary that you're paying them to sit at home, do nothing! (*Shhh* ... it's unlikely they'll file a claim.)

There is always that possibility that if you say, "You may leave today," the employee will call their new employer, who might agree to start the employee the next day. In this case, you have no unemployment exposure at all.

Things to Know Before They Go

For any kind of exit from the organization, you need to check your state regulations regarding when the final wage/salary payment is due. Sometimes, you are required to present exiting employees with their final pay at the exit interview, particularly in a termination situation. There are only a few states that require this, but be sure you know if you are in one of those states.

You should conduct an exit interview whenever you are able.

You should conduct an exit interview whenever you are able. The purpose of an exit interview is to find out what you're doing right and what you can do better. There are some things you can't change — you can only pay what you can pay — but if people are leaving because they think the office environment is stifling, or because their ideas are always shot down, you can immediately start to address those issues with the employees you still have.

When possible, have someone neutral conduct the exit interview. It should never, ever, *ever* be conducted by the supervisor. I've started doing exit interviews online, so consider this an unpaid plug for SurveyMonkey. What's great about an online survey is that you can send it to employees after they've gone (and after they've had time to distance themselves a little). It's important to find out why someone has left — why they *really* left. We have also started to ask them when they *began* looking for a new job; remember, they probably didn't just start looking when this new opportunity presented itself — the root of the problem was in advance of the actual resignation.

Don't just collect your exit interviews and file them away. Collect and analyze the data — another reason something like SurveyMonkey is so great. Depending on what version you have, some survey tools will organize and tabulate the data in meaningful ways for you, making your analysis of the data and subsequent decision-making more intuitive and easy.

The reason you're doing an exit interview is to find out what you're doing right and what you can do better. Let your employees give you a little clarity on their way out the door, as a final parting gift.

⚠️ A Word About Resignations During a Business Disruption

Ahh, the "Great Resignation."[1] Trust me, it's real. It's not just a social media "thing." It exists and it has happened across the U.S. Did COVID-19 cause this? I honestly don't believe it was the cause *but* I believe it was the straw that broke the proverbial camel's back. Look how hard a majority of people were working prior to March 2020 — "do more with less" was almost a motto for employers and employees alike. Guess what? That gets old. Our society worked hard, played hard, and moved fast. Then — BAM — we were forced to slow down. We were all forced to reexamine a LOT of areas in our work lives and home lives.

Regardless of the reason why the Great Resignation struck, it happened. Masses of people quit their jobs. Personally? I believe we all learned to live with less and we learned how valuable slowing down was for our health, our families, and our sanity.

What's a company to do to prevent this from happening again?

- Focus on culture, not necessarily cash
- Hold underperformers accountable because our good performers see what "they" get away with
- Put in good employee-relations practices
- Implement fair but consistent HR practices, regardless of the size of the company

1 https://en.wikipedia.org/wiki/Great_Resignation

- Be honest — always be honest with your employees

- Hear what your employees are saying — that doesn't mean you have to implement every idea they have but don't you like to be heard? Don't *you* feel valued when someone listens to your input?

These tips are simply good business practice to reduce turnover, even in good times. You don't even need to wait for an emergency to step up!

Chapter Seventeen
After They've Gone

Your former employees may be out of sight, but they should never be out of mind. They're part of the institutional history of your organization forever. Learn from them.

And beyond what you and your team can learn from departures, there are sometimes silver linings. Farewell is not always "good riddance." On the positive side, if employees left of their own accord but had a positive experience with your company, you may find yourself working with them again in a freelance or consulting capacity.

At the very least, they'll be a great brand ambassador for you. If and when possible, maintain a positive relationship going forward.

Beyond freelance connections and word-of-mouth referrals, former employees who resign and move on professionally may ultimately be a perfect fit for you again in the future. Sometimes the best new hire is someone who's already worked for you — think of the time you would save in onboarding alone! If the right position becomes available, consider former employees who have left amicably. Former employees can be outstanding prospective employees because:

- They already have a relationship with you and may have maintained bonds with other employees, customers, and clients

- They have existing knowledge of the company and the company culture, and
- While out in the world working for other people, they will have gained new skills and ideas that they can now bring back to share with you, enriching your company's depth of knowledge and experience and even growing your list of contacts and possible clients.

In HR, we call these people "boomerang employees" and we love them!

Let Go With Grace, But Cover Your Bases

It's human nature for you to take it personally when employees resign, but don't. Wish them well. Throw them a going-away luncheon and congratulate them when you announce it to the rest of the company. "Hey, George is pursuing other opportunities. We appreciate everything that he did for us while he was here, and we wish him well in the future."

Letting someone go with grace sends the message to your remaining employees that you care about them and their happiness. You want to be a good employer, but no job is a fit for everybody. And, there isn't always an opportunity for someone to rise up through the ranks of a company. Don't forget that your employees are on their own journeys, too — sometimes it's just time for them to make a leap to a new industry, a new profession, a return to college, or a geographic move. It's not always "personal" when employees move on.

> **Letting someone go with grace sends the message to your remaining employees that you care about them and their happiness.**

Following a termination, resignation, or retirement, you want to make sure that you've retrieved all company property. I recommend getting it all at once — keys, credit cards, badges — anything and everything you can think of, so you don't have to keep going after ex-employees for things. Less official contact is better when it comes to terminated employees, even when the split was friendly.

If there is any risk of volatility, instability, retribution, or retaliation from ex-employees, consider the relatively inexpensive cost of changing all the locks and issuing new keys versus the cost of having to buy all new computers after those disgruntled ex-employees come back and smash things to pieces. Protecting yourself, your business, and your current employees is definitely worth every penny.

In the case of a company credit card, you can always call the credit card company and cancel an ex-employee's card (or the whole account, if necessary). You may want to do this as a matter of standard practice, considering how easy it is to store information and buy things without needing an actual card in hand.

As for former employees maintaining connections to your business, it's impossible to keep your staff from continuing their friendships with former coworkers, so don't even try. Whether someone resigned, retired, or was fired, chances are they still have relationships with people on your staff and are often connected through social media.

Sometimes, a former employee will use friends still on staff to dig for information, even if it's just a way to remain connected. Remind employees that, while they may still be friends, that person is no longer an employee and that information related to the internal workings of the company are no longer their business. Legally, you can give your employees guidelines, but nothing is enforceable unless you have a confidentiality agreement of some sort, or the information is protected under law.

In the case of an involuntary termination, there is absolutely nothing wrong with telling your employees, "If so-and-so reaches out to you, please let us know." You should also remind them that if the former employee's contact makes them at all uncomfortable, they should let you know right away so you can help.

I discourage current employees from initiating contact with former employees, but it's going to happen — they want to make sure that their friend is all right. Again, you can give guidelines to help keep things professional; just be careful that you're not propping open a door to a vindictive or volatile ex-employee.

The hardest thing for any organization is to remember that when a former employee comes back to visit, they're a visitor. If your visitors must be escorted around your building, then your former employee must be escorted. It's hard to enforce because old habits kick in, but it's truly a protective measure for both you and that former employee. Consider the seemingly innocuous situation in which a retiree stops by; if they chat for five minutes with this person, and five minutes with that person, they can effectively take hours away from the collective workday. My suggestion is that you manage those visits. Invite them back for lunch on a Friday or have them join the staff for a get-together after work.

It can be especially difficult for retirees to make the break from their colleagues after working with these same people for 20, 30, or even 40 years. Sitting at home, they might not know what to do with themselves. Be gracious but be firm. Let them know you're glad to see them, then be sure to show them the appropriate way to move forward.

People may move on from the company, but we still need to respect and appreciate that they were an employee of ours and played a part in our organization. We also must respect their privacy, their dignity, and their future. They have a right to carry on and to make a living. As long as you manage those relationships with respect, you'll be fine.

A Word About Former Employees During a Business Disruption

In the wake of the initial disruptions caused by COVID-19, several of my clients had former employees who had a difficult time receiving their unemployment checks. Just because they are "former" employees did not mean we should simply say "Sorry, that's your problem." In this situation, particularly in central PA, there was not much we could do but we still tried. You can write letters; you can provide "back doors" for your former employees. In many instances, we helped them find out who their local representatives were so they could get some "bigger" assistance.

At the end of the day, even in an emergency, former employees are always valued stakeholders because they used to be valued employees. Do what you can to assist and, if you are unable to help, be honest and be empathetic. Who knows if and when you may need that individual back to work?

Case Study
Seeing the ROI from Good HR Practices

As we near the end of this book, you might be looking at your scribbled notes in the margins or your sticky notes on the pages (or your highlights and comment bubbles if you're reading the Kindle edition!), thinking, "Based on what I've learned here, I have a lot of changes I need to implement and ideas I want to try! But do I have the time … or the money? Will the hard work pay off?"

The answer is *yes*. There truly is a return on investment (ROI) when you implement solid HR practices. Those returns could come from any number of places, and some may be hard to measure, but here are just four examples of the kinds of results we see when smart HR practices are put into place:

- Improved customer service
- Lower absenteeism
- Reduced workers' compensation claims
- Decreased turnover

I've told you a lot about how we do things at HR Resolutions and have shared some "anonymous" examples from some of our clients. But you might be curious about how it all comes together at one organization that's dedicated to the value of HR. Thus, this case study.

Let me introduce Facility Concierge Services (FCS) as an ideal example of "things done right" with a measurable return on investment as a result. Here is their story ...

Started in 2014, **Facility Concierge Services, LLC**, is a professional, commercial cleaning service focusing on high-end office space in Central Pennsylvania. FCS is committed to making sure their clients consistently receive clean offices from their professional crews. "We pay attention to details which allow you to focus on your core business." [1] But instead of focusing the majority of her external branding and promotional efforts on customer development and new clients (as many business owners do), FCS's owner, Mary Calverley, focuses her marketing dollars on recruitment and retention! Her target is to find the *right* employees and then to treat those employees right. Your first thought of a cleaning service may be that a group of janitors come into the building in the dark of night and, poof, your building is clean. Calverley sees it differently — her team is composed of cleaning technicians (*not* janitors) with set, early evening hours (i.e., no "dark of the night") scheduled throughout the work week. FCS also employs Day Porters for their larger clients with consistent cleaning and service needs.

FCS uses a variety of unique systems to find and retain that "niche" employee who shares common values that match the core values intrinsic to the company:

- Be sincere
- Treat others right
- Finish what we start
- Never give up

---

[1] http://www.facility-concierge.com/

- Get better every day

FCS also consistently gives back to the community through supporting employees in 5K fundraisers, as well as other charity events. Calverley and her area managers are less worried about someone's work history than they are about their core values being a fit — that's one of the ways she knows they'll stay!

Retention Should Start at Recruiting

Calverley is recruiting for the same part-time folks that every other company is trying to reach. But she has an average of three interviewees a week attending her group interviews (she actually had 10 participants at one!). And she doesn't stop recruiting — even if there are no current openings. If she finds a Rock Star, she hires them! She wants to be sure she is always sufficiently staffed!

What's different?

Notice that I said "group interview," which is a somewhat unique concept for small business owners. First, Calverley uses a reminder system to keep the candidate engaged in the interview process, from the time they respond to an ad, until they have completed the group interview. The system "touches" the candidate six times before they walk in the door; these touchpoints are a mix of emails, telephone calls, and texts. Every "touch" provides the candidate an opportunity to cancel, without having to speak with anyone.

Interviews start promptly at 5:30 p.m. (Hmm, the same time as the working shift begins!) She turns interviewees away if they arrive after 5:30 p.m., unless they made previous arrangements with her.

The group interview provides FCS the opportunity to evaluate these candidates from the very beginning. The initial questions are basic in nature:

- What do you know about the company?
- Why us?

Calverley has learned this is the best use of her time, while it provides her an opportunity to evaluate both how the candidates interact with others, as well as to determine their patience level because proper cleaning is *not* a fast job!

Once the group interview is complete, selected candidates will move on to a one-on-one interview (usually on the phone). Calverley has learned not to hire on the spot ... she wants to give the candidate time to properly reflect upon what they've learned during the interview process.

When a candidate is extended an offer with FCS, they initially are categorized as a "Rock Star in Training." Calverley (with some help from her friends at HR Resolutions) developed the Rock Star Program as part of their training, development, and retention goals for the company. Employees advance through various "Rock Star" levels through training, attendance, and demonstration of the company's core values. Some levels even require written tests to advance. The program also includes procedures in which employees are recognized through company shout outs and with gift items like embroidered jackets, trophies and paid time off!

FCS ROCK ST★R LEVELS

- Rock Star in Training
- Bronze Rock Star
- Silver Rock Star
- Gold Rock Star
- Platinum Rock Star
- Diamond Rock Star

So, what else does Calverley do for her employees? A whole lot that employees truly appreciate, like:

- Birthdays — Shout out on the group board at the office, and a personal card
- Anniversaries — Shout out (including pictures and social media) and cards
- Perfect Attendance for a Month — Shout out
    - At one year, Granite Rock Star statuette plus cash (which increases with each consecutive month of perfect attendance)
    - In August of 2019, FCS awarded 26 perfect attendance awards out of a staff of 50.
- Loyalty Bonuses
- Above & Beyond Awards — Management determined, and employees get their choice of a gift card
- Annual Summer Picnic for employees and their families
- Pumpkin Pies for Thanksgiving

- Holiday Gift
- Employee Referral Program — Choice of gift card after the referred employee's 90th day

When asked why she does so much — and with such passion — to recruit and retain great employees, Mary's first answer was "I'm crazy." In reality, her "why" is that she needs to retain her talent in an industry where turnover is between 200% and 400%!)[2]

> **Facility Concierge Service Turnover?**
>
> 105.7% — which means their competitors have at least twice as much turnover as they do (if not three or four times as many). Yep, I ran those FCS turnover numbers myself (i.e., they were *not* supplied by Calverley, or the staff of FCS, as I have access to their employee Human Resource Information System). Pretty remarkable.

And to double check the "numbers," our office recently completed an employee survey. Highlights include:

- 18% of the respondents had been with the company longer than 5 years
- 36% are between the ages of 26 to 35
- 55% believe the organization provided sufficient New Hire training
- 91% indicated they can trust what the organization tells them

---

[2] "Combatting Cleaning Industry Turnover" November 30, 2018, Vanguard Cleaning Systems of the Southern Valley. https://www.vanguardsv.com/2018/11/combatting-cleaning-industry-turnover/

- **100% agree that "senior management communicates appropriately with staff"**
- **100% agree that "Mary acknowledges good work"**
- **A Net Promoter Score (NPS) of 100**, indicating that all survey respondents gave a 10 (on a scale of 1 to 10) on their likelihood to recommend FCS as a place to work
- 55% plan to continue working with FCS for at least another 2 years

From someone who has conducted a *lot* of employee surveys, I found these responses to be AMAZING!

Things That Set Facility Concierge Services (FCS) Apart:

- Cleaning technicians (*not* janitors)
- Group interviews
- Pre-interview touchpoints
- Rock Star program from day one
- Perks and recognition that few full-time employees at other similar companies receive

For small businesses that really thrive, HR can't be an afterthought or a "check the box" set of processes and requirements. Good HR practices that generate ROI must be woven into the very cultural fabric of an organization and be championed from the top. At FCS, Mary Calverley works hard to make the culture and environment such that employees *want* to stay. Unlike other similar companies, FCS doesn't tolerate no call/no shows or infighting between employees. She understands that to treat her customers properly, she can't function if she's constantly burning through people. She cares about getting the right people in the first place, and treating them well, recognizing their efforts, and keeping them for the long term.

You, too, can have a positive return from putting the right HR practices in place. You don't have to implement all of the ideas that inspire FCS, nor do you need to follow all the steps in this book. But choose one thing to improve or one place where you'd like to excel, and get started. Talk to your employees — find YOUR one thing that you and your employees can be passionate about, and do that. And next year, add a second or third thing. You don't have to eat the entire elephant in one seating! Growing a business, and growing in your HR expertise, is a process that takes time. But there's no better time to start than now.

Talk to your employees — find YOUR one thing that you and your employees can be passionate about, and do that.

Conclusion
Failure to Plan Is Planning to Fail

The best HR management comes from planning, however simple, then conveying it honestly and clearly to your staff. The best HR managers — accidental or otherwise — actively listen to their employees, engage in interactive dialogues to solve problems, and work steadily and swiftly to ensure and maintain a safe work environment. They hold honest conversations and they encourage management to be real.

The best HR managers — accidental or otherwise — actively listen to their employees, engage in interactive dialogues to solve problems, and work steadily and swiftly to ensure and maintain a safe work environment.

Employees who work under a top-notch "accidental HR manager" are crystal clear on their job descriptions and how their positions relate to the success of the company. They understand and connect to the mission, vision, and values of the company, and they treat coworkers with respect.

We keep returning to a few key themes in this book: honesty, clarity, respect, and the need to *document, document, document.* Let those four themes guide you as you begin to implement these best practices at your own company. While your employees might bristle at the first changes, those four themes will help bring everyone on board.

Don't feel the need to implement everything in this book all at once. Rushing into things headfirst will only create more problems. Instead, plan to implement one section of this book at a time, keeping these themes, or guiding principles, in mind.

Honesty

This is where you walk the talk. Create the environment that you would love to work in. If you were an employee, would you want to work at your company? If the answer isn't yes, then go back to your mission, vision, and values, and start there. Bring yourself into alignment with your own expectations; that's the best way to be an honest leader. Create the kind of company where you would thrive as an employee, and then find others who will thrive in that environment. It's okay if that's not everybody, and it's okay if current staff members choose to move on as you get your house in order.

If you were an employee, would you want to work at your company? Create the kind of company where you would thrive as an employee, and then find others who will thrive in that environment.

Clarity

If there is *only* one thing that you can do for your HR program, I recommend that you start by getting your job descriptions in order. They are truly the hub of the wheel, and everything else stems from those job descriptions. Even if that's the *only* thing you do, it will have an immediate impact and will start to affect every other aspect of your organization in a positive way. You, as the owner or manager, will have a better understanding of how everything fits together and flows, just from implementing this one foundational change. Your employees will feel that shift, too. Make sure your employees understand their job descriptions and watch the subtle changes that begin to take place in the company culture.

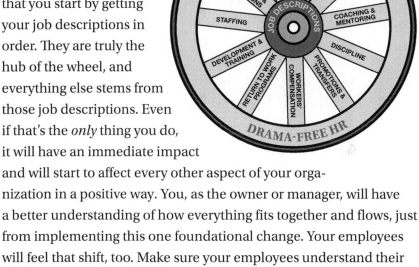

Respect

The other thing to do right away is to implement the Golden Rule — treating people the way that you would like to be treated. As cliché as this sounds, it provides clear goals and guidelines, such as speaking in a respectful tone, thanking others for their contributions, calmly coaching and mentoring when things go wrong, giving others the benefit of the doubt, and listening to suggestions and concerns.

Document, Document, Document

Get in the habit of keeping notes, tracking changes, and collecting data. You can start documenting today, even before you put together your job descriptions. Pull up your calendar right now and make a note: "Decided to rewrite job descriptions and start documenting good and bad incidents at work." Figure out a system, however simple, and get started. It doesn't have to be fancy to be functional.

Focus on What Matters Most

Think about what you would like your company to be remembered for, beyond the products you sell and the services you provide.

- Are you here to provide a quality work environment where your employees can thrive as individuals while working on a team?
- Do you want your employees to have a healthy work-life balance?
- Do you want your employees to be proud to work for you and your company?
- Do you want your company to be known for the good work it does in the community, or for the educational opportunities it provides for your staff members and their families?

Figure out what matters most to you. Share your excitement and passion with your staff. Find out what matters to them. See if you're in alignment. Let that knowledge influence how you walk forward into the future, together: a united team with an exceptional leader.

Figure out what matters most to you. Share your excitement and passion with your staff. Find out what matters to them. See if you're in alignment. Let that knowledge influence how you walk forward into the future, together: a united team with an exceptional leader.

Not everybody believes that HR is fun, but it's always been one of my company's core values. We believe it. We're passionate about it. We love it. We breathe it. If someone doesn't get that, they are not going to be successful at HR Resolutions. We may not be curing cancer, but HR is still serious stuff — it's where you clarify your business ethics and set them down in print. It's the heart and soul of your values that keep your company moving forward with employees who are whole and healthy, happy and productive, and free of the drama that bogs so many companies down.

Ben Franklin said, "If you fail to plan, you are planning to fail." You may have accidentally ended up in HR, but you no longer have to bumble along, causing more distractions and putting your business and employees at risk.

Far from it! You now have more than the basic requirements for moving forward in HR — in fact, you have the makings of a Master's degree in HR with a good grasp of best practices. Having clarity on your HR role is going to set your organization apart from your competitors. Frankly, that's what this is all about — finding a way to set yourself apart, so you can draw the best candidates who will make the best employees, do the best work, and help your company grow.

There is nothing better than hearing the joy in a new employee's voice when you offer them a job that they really want. That joy continues as they flourish in a position that is a perfect fit for them and for your company. That joy can continue for years or decades, and even as they make a change and move on ... because you know exactly what you're going to do to bring in the next candidate for that position, so that you and your company can continue to shine.

And that joy starts with drama-free HR.

P.S. Don't forget to plan for the next disruption. May it never come but ... if it does, let's be better prepared than we all were for COVID-19!

Acknowledgments

So many people to thank ...

- It may sound odd coming from an HR professional, but **I must thank God** for every one of my successes and all the blessings in my life.

- Thank you **to my parents, John and Mary Ellen Milliken**, who raised me to believe I could do anything I set my mind to. I hope I've done them proud.

- A special thank you to my dad, for teaching me work ethic.

- **To Barry Young, the best husband ever** and a truly extraordinary man. He's my best friend. He grounds me, he spoils me terribly, and he believes in me.

- My thanks **to Phyllis Webber, Ron McKinley, and Jerry Hiler** — three managers who saw something in me a long, long time ago.

- **Dave Guelcher** — you were in the mix too; may you and **Mike Fogt** rest in peace. You were both my first HR mentors ... way back in the day.

- Thank you **to Glenn Ames**, who made me go out and talk to people I didn't know and tell them about this funny little idea I had for a business.

- **To Ryan Keith**, formerly with the Harrisburg Regional Chamber and Capital Region Economic Development Corporation, who said (about the concept of HR Resolutions), "Wow, what a great idea!" all the way back in 2004.

- **A huge thanks to my staff** (past, present, and future), for following me and embracing our mission.

- **To Maria Diaz,** of Order and Ease, you always have my back. Thanks for jumping in at the last minute for proof reading!

- **To Brian Carberry** with Growth Coaching, who asks me the tough questions that I don't want to answer — LOL — but who makes be a better person, not just a better business person!

- A heartfelt thank you **to my clients**, without whom I couldn't follow my passion.

- **To Peter Margaritis, CSP, CPA**, who introduced me to Kate Colbert.

- And **to Kate Colbert, George Stevens, and the entire staff at Silver Tree Publishing** — every one of them has believed in me and heard the author inside!

Go Beyond the Book

If you enjoyed what you learned from *Honest and Real* and could use some help auditing your practices or implementing thoughtful HR practices, Karen Young and HR Resolutions would be honored to help. There's not project too small or too big!

Hire Karen to:

- Create a savvy HR strategy for you

- Discuss challenging and simple HR and employee relations issues

- Review your current handbook or create a new one for you

- Become your HR department

- Create effective job descriptions

- Conduct HR training on crucial issues, like unlawful harassment, interviewing skills, and how to have courageous, honest, and real conversations at work

Get the conversation started at 717-652-5187 or Karen@HonestAndRealHR.com.

We Are:

- Easy to work with
- Reasonably priced
- Champions of #DramaFreeHR

Our Mission:

We work side by side with our client partners, helping them create workplaces where employees WANT to come to work — every day!

Our Core Values:

- Going the extra mile for our clients is second nature to us.
- ALWAYS do right — no matter what.
- Paying our "community rent" isn't considered work.
- HR is FUN!
- We "get it" (things aren't always black and white; our clients do have a business to run).

Keep in Touch

Learn more about Karen Young, HR Resolutions, and the material in this book:

HRResolutions.com
HonestAndRealHR.com

Send an email:

Karen@HonestAndRealHR.com

Find, follow, share, and engage on social media:

Facebook.com/HRResolutions
Facebook.com/Groups/HRResolutions
Twitter.com/HRResolutions
LinkedIn.com/in/HRResolutions

Mail or ship something special to:

Karen Young
HR Resolutions
4075 Linglestown Rd
PMB 256
Harrisburg PA 17112

To order books in bulk and learn about quantity discounts:

Interested in ordering 25 or more copies of *Honest and Real* for your organization, association, or conference, or to distribute to clients who are business owners and leaders? Send Karen an email at Karen@HonestAndRealHR.com.

About the Author

Karen A. Young, SPHR, SHRM-SCP, has made a career of going the extra mile for the people she serves, inspiring others to always do what is right (even when it's not always easy), and finding joy and FUN in the practice of human resources. Karen is the founder and president of HR Resolutions, a full-service human resource management company, where she and her team help clients — in a variety of industries and in organizations of all sizes — create savvy strategies and develop solutions that produce real results.

Founder & President of HR Resolutions, Karen recognized professionally through SHRM as a Senior Professional in HR (SHRM-SPR) and through the HRCI as a Senior Professional in HR (SPHR). She has also been recognized as one of Pennsylvania's Best 50 Women in Business, and AGS ranked HR Resolutions as a Best HR Consulting Company in 2021. *Central Penn Business Journal* honored HR Resolutions in 2020 as a Game Changer—one of Central PA's most dynamic and impactful businesses and leaders. Karen regularly contributes HR insights and strategy nationwide to SHRM, *USA Today*, and ZipRecruiter.

Karen is a sought-after speaker, trainer, and consultant best known for her training programs on unlawful harassment, interviewing, and how to have courageous conversations in the workplace. She is well-regarded as a business partner with an unflagging work ethic and a passion for helping business leaders say "yes" to their people by better understanding the risks and rewards of running a business where leaders can focus on what they need to accomplish ... all within a thoughtful HR framework.

Karen holds a Bachelor of Science in Business Administration and Psychology from Lebanon Valley College and a Master of Arts in Industrial Relations from Saint Francis University. She lives in Harrisburg, PA, with her husband, Barry, and their retired greyhounds. *Honest and Real: An Essential Guidebook for Drama-Free Human Resources* is based on her first book, *Stop Knocking on My Door: Drama-Free HR to Help Grow Your Business* (first edition, 2015, and second edition, 2020), reimagined and republished in 2022 for a post-pandemic world. She is also the author of *Sought-After: What It Takes to Be Heard, Be Trusted, and Be Recognized for Your Expertise.*

Made in United States
Orlando, FL
30 January 2023

29200404R10159